KII OURSELVES TO LIVE

COLON CANCER AND ME

WRITTEN BY A. GABRIEL

This paperback edition was published in Great Britain by A. Gabriel publishing in 2024.

Paperback ISBN: 978-1-0687916-5-9.

Cover and illustrations by A. Gabriel.

About the author

The author was born in the East Midlands and is in his late 50s. For decades, he has been involved in company turnarounds and restructures all over the UK, basically putting companies back on their feet when they have fallen on difficult times for whatever reason.

Having retired in his mid-fifties, he found time to allocate to one of his personal interests: the climate crisis. The choice to write a book about it was somewhat unusual, as he had never written a book before and had failed English as a subject at school due to a lack of interest; however, he had written numerous commercial trading agreements between companies that he had worked for and some of the largest companies in the world.

These documents could be thirty or more pages long, contain numerous appendices, and form a legally binding agreement between the companies concerned.

This ability was born through the analysis required when studying a company's problems, which led to the development of a logical, focused, and analytical mindset. This mindset hasn't changed and has been used throughout his life.

When dealing with a company that is struggling, every decision is important, as a bad decision could finish an ailing company, whereas it would only hinder a prosperous one; therefore, every decision needed to be calculated and correct.

With the use of a grammar checker, as well as pestering his partner, and after more than 2,000 hours of research and writing, he produced a book that contained over four hundred A4 pages, which was said to be more like a thesis than a book. The more he read, the more he understood that humanity's problem was much bigger than just the climate. In fact, it was equally as big a problem, if not bigger. The problem was pollution and how it was affecting mankind.

Writing the first book allowed him to fill some gaps in this book in relation to why cancer was becoming so prevalent in our societies.

The author is now looking to split the original book into a series of books marketed under the leading title of 'Killing Ourselves to Live' with Colon Cancer and Me being the first in the series.

The Cancer Screening Trust

A special thank you to everyone at The Cancer Screening Trust for all their help and advice during such difficult times.

Website: https://www.thecancerscreeningtrust.co.uk/

Testing and general enquiries: Tel: 01935 725005

Email: hello@thecancerscreeningtrust.co.uk

They are a not-for-profit organisation (15/05/24).

I found them very helpful - a good sounding board when my head was full of questions and fear. I particularly found their free consultation via video link very simple and an easy way of communicating.

When I was looking to have a private MRI scan, I found communicating with The Cancer Screening Trust very easy. I spoke to a consultant directly via video link and was confident that I would be dealt with properly and that my questions would be answered.

This book has been written in thanks and in tribute to all the medical staff who I was fortunate enough to have looking after me: from my doctor who put me on a two-week pathway; to the people who looked after me during my colonoscopies; to the consultant who ensured that I was put into a COVID-free hospital for my operation; to the nurse who was assigned to me on my admission to the hospital; to the surgeons who carried out my operation; to the colorectal nurses who kept an eye on me during my journey; and to anyone else involved with my diagnosis, investigations, operations, and recuperation, my heartfelt thanks.

It is also a testament to my loving partner, to whom I owe my life, and to those friends who gave me the encouragement that I needed while going through chemotherapy; it meant the world to me. Thank you so much.

In loving memory of 'Magic Molly,' a wonderful mother.

Contents

Prologue

As you will have guessed from the title of the book, I have had colon cancer, or bowel cancer, as it is also called. I am pleased to now be able to use the word 'had' rather than 'have' to describe my current position in relation to cancer. I wrote this book to help people who have been diagnosed with this specific cancer, as well as their family and friends, as it is useful for those around the person who has been diagnosed with cancer to know what it is about and what could lie ahead both mentally and physically.

To be diagnosed with any cancer is an immediate shock, so I wanted to write about my experience in the hope that it would help people appreciate that there can be light at the end of the tunnel and that you can come out of it in one piece.

I will take you through my journey and try to explain what happens, why it happens, the different operations that can take place depending on where the cancer is, the equipment used during the investigations and during the operation itself, as well as give what I found to be useful tips in handling various situations that may occur.

I wondered whether to write the book initially, as medical staff told me not to listen to anyone else, as everyone's experience and outcome can be different. This can include how fast they recover, any changes they may have to live with, to how they cope with chemotherapy and its side-effects, if indeed they need it.

My mind was changed by conversations that I had with people who'd had cancer and who appeared to be struggling mentally with what was happening and what had happened to them. After talking to them, they seemed to be better for it, so I decided that I would write about my experience in the hope that it helps others. I hope it does and that you find it insightful and helpful.

I have written it in layman's terms, as one thing that I noticed was that the medical reports that were being sent to me had an awful lot of medical terminology in them. This book tells it how it is, warts and all, and gives examples and explanations of what you will and may come across.

One thing to bear in mind is that this is about my journey and treatment and the medication that I had in relation to the type of cancer that I had. There are numerous types of bowel cancer, each with their own symptoms, treatments, and medications, which can often be dependent on the patient's health, any existing ailments, and their level of fitness. You can even get bowel cancer in the small intestine, although it is rare. This is just one example of one journey, which was extended when it spread to my liver.

As you will have read, my background is business based and not medical based. I have written this book to try and help people understand what having cancer is like, how it can be life changing or even life ending, and to explain how it is looking to be a part of all of our lives, whether we like it or not.

Information has been taken from numerous sources, and there is a reference section at the back, allowing you to look at whatever topic is of interest to you.

As you will read, I made countless assumptions during my journey, a lot of which were wrong. Some of those assumptions could have done me harm if I had carried them out on my own without discussing them with medical staff first.

I say it many times: this is about my journey; everyone's can be different; therefore, always speak with your medical team relating to any queries that you have or actions that you think you or they should be taking.

I readily admit to making numerous assumptions throughout my journey and being wrong. I will now research a question that I have to try and understand it better, and I will then have a conversation with my consultant or a colorectal nurse about it.

1

Discovery of my cancer and initial investigations

Before we get into the nitty-gritty, I will admit to not being a fan of medical terminology; therefore, I will use the following terms of reference when being used in relation to body parts: bottom = anus, wiener = penis, pee = urine, and stool = solid excreta (poo). I am sure that I will be frowned upon by medics for using such terminology, but at the end of the day, I need to feel comfortable with what I write.

Well, how did I know or find out that I had cancer, specifically bowel cancer? To my knowledge, I had no telltale symptoms apart from sloppy, odorous stools for a while, but that was five or more years ago; it was pure luck that it was found. I know that you are meant to go to your GP should you notice a change in your bowel habits, but if everyone did that, I thought they would be overrun.

The main symptoms to look out for are: blood in your stools or coming from your bottom; a lump or pain in your abdomen or stomach; an unknown source or reason for weight loss and tiredness; and a change in bowel habits (frequency, constipation, or diarrhoea, which may come and go), which are different from normal [1].

Having read the above paragraph, I suppose I should have gone to my GP, but I didn't want to waste my doctor's time if it had just been down to a poor diet or an upset stomach.

There is always an excuse for not making that call, isn't there? Now that I understand the ramifications of not doing so, I would wholeheartedly recommend contacting your GP if you have any such symptoms. It can be as easy as sending you a test kit, taking a sample, and then popping it in the post for analysis. An early diagnosis could save the NHS time and money in the long run, as well as provide you with a much better prognosis.

My 'journey' started when I received a test kit from the NHS in 2021. I was very lucky in that they had only started to send kits out to people my age in April 2021 [2]; therefore, bearing in mind when I received mine, I must have been one of the first to receive it of my age. Unfortunately, stupidly, it stayed on the kitchen worktop for several weeks; I was foolishly going to throw it in the bin! Can you remember the ads explaining that it is better to diagnose cancer or the symptoms of it sooner rather than later? Thankfully, my partner kept on telling me to get it done and to send it off; I duly did as I was told!

The test kit that I was sent was very simple. All I had to do was stick a small spike into one of my stools, pop it into a container, and send it off. It took five minutes. Five minutes to save a life!

Around this time, my pee came out a pink colour (just the once), meaning that there was most likely blood in it. Blood in your pee can be an indicator of cancer, along with other possible problems relating to your urinary tract [3]. I went to my GP, who immediately put me on a two-week pathway.

This is basically a system designed to get you a hospital appointment within a short space of time (two weeks), should there be an indication of cancer or another serious condition [4].

Around this time, I received a letter relating to the stool sample that I had sent off. To my horror, the letter confirmed that they had found microscopic traces of blood in my sample. So now, not only have I peed blood, but blood has also been found in my stool sample. This was really not what I wanted to hear.

From here, I was sent down two separate paths as I had two separate results: one to do with blood in my pee (known as haematuria), which could indicate bladder cancer or a number of other problems [5], and the other to do with blood in my stool, which is an indicator of bowel cancer, amongst other things. Even though I had two symptoms that were indicators of cancer, it still could have been something else. By no means was a cancer diagnosis cast in stone.

My first visit to the hospital was due to the fact that I had peed blood. I had a number of scans looking at my bladder, gallbladder, testes, kidneys, and prostate, which all turned out to be fine. There were, however, a few co-morbidities found: a cyst on one of my epididymides (in the scrotum), a polyp in my gallbladder, and haemorrhoids. I was assured that none of them were seen as problems. These checks were carried out by ultrasound, which is a non-invasive procedure.

As well as the ultrasound, I had what is known as a flexible cystoscopy. This is an invasive procedure, as it entails inserting an apparatus about the thickness of a pencil into your urethra all the way into your bladder. On entering my bladder, it felt like I was going to wet myself; it is just a feeling that you are warned you might experience. The cystoscope had a form of camera and a light on the end linked to a screen, enabling me to watch it worm its way along my urethra and into my bladder. I am afraid that with procedures like this, there is no room for modesty or shyness; it is a case of gritting your teeth and thinking of England!

For me, one of the worst parts of this procedure was the numbing of my wiener - I found it extremely painful. An anaesthetic gel was applied to the tip of my wiener to numb the area, allowing the insertion of the cystoscope.

When I was young (in my teens), I used to experiment with things, and one time I put toothpaste on the end of my wiener – please don't ask me why. It took a second or two before I started jumping up and down, screaming, and trying to wipe it off. The burning sensation was horrendous. I can only liken the application of the anaesthetic to this, but thankfully the anaesthetic did its job in a few seconds and numbed the area, whereas the toothpaste was absorbed into the skin, meaning that the burning continued for quite some time!

Another time, when I was very young, I stuck my wiener in melted tar on a telegraph pole, and my mother had to scrub it off with soap and a nail brush. Needless to say, neither of us were very happy, and it has never been the same colour since! It must be a fetish for me!

The outcome of the cystoscopy was fine; my bladder showed no signs of cancer. A friend of mine, who admits to having a relatively low pain threshold, had the same procedure. When the anaesthetic gel was applied, he said that he started screaming. It was only when he left the consulting room after the procedure that he realised the room he was in was right next to the waiting room. We both had a good laugh at the thought of the people who were sitting waiting for the same procedure, listening to him shouting and whaling in agony. In instances like this, of which there are a number, you have to find the funny side - something to laugh at, even if it is at yourself.

After the procedure, I cleaned myself up and went for a pee. I thought the anaesthetic was painful; I hadn't banked on going for a pee being even more painful, but then again, it is not every day you get something the width of a pencil inserted into your wiener and pushed along your urethra. It hurt so much that I struggled to pee, as the pain stopped me from doing so. Thankfully, it didn't take too long to wear off and return to normal.

Not long after this, I went to my GP to have a blood sample taken by one of the nurses. The sample was then sent by courier to the hospital the next day for analysis.

The second main visit to the hospital was to have a colonoscopy; this was done after I had a consultation to explain what it entailed and what they were looking for. A colonoscopy is the rectal equivalent of a flexible cystoscopy, but instead of inserting the scope into your wiener, the apparatus is inserted into your bottom and is then manipulated along the large colon.

The large colon starts at the caecum, which is where the small intestine (also known as the small bowel or small colon) meets the large colon; this is on your right-hand side. From the caecum, the large colon travels upwards (ascending colon) and then across your body (transverse colon) to your left- hand side, where it then travels down (descending colon) to meet the sigmoid colon, which is just before your rectum, which leads to your bottom.

The apparatus used is called a colonoscope and is similar to a cystoscope in that it has a light and a video camera attached at one end and is linked to a screen. Both of these apparatuses can also have various attachments on them to enable the endoscopist (the person carrying out the procedure) to perform such things as a biopsy or the removal of a polyp. A biopsy is the removal of a small sample of tissue, which is sent away for analysis.

Before I had a colonoscopy, I had to clear my bowels so that when the scope was inserted, it could see everything and not be obscured by forming stools and coloured water. I was sent a package from the NHS with a couple of sachets of laxatives in it. Instructions on how and when to take them, what I could eat, when I should stop eating, and what I could drink before the colonoscopy were also included. I actually stopped eating a day before I was instructed to try and ensure that the endoscopist could get the clearest images possible due to my bowel being completely empty.

I mixed the powder from the sachets with water as instructed. The sachet said that it was mango flavour, which I thought sounded nice - at least an attempt had been made to make it taste nice. Unfortunately, no matter how much I stirred it, there were still undissolved particles in it. I started to drink it as per the instructions, spreading my consumption throughout the day.

The mix turned out to be quite thick with regards to consistency and had a strange smell about it; I also found it to be salty. All in all, it was not a very nice experience, and that was just drinking it! I mixed the powder with fizzy water in the hope that it would make it a bit more palatable, which it did.

I sat in the living room watching a programme on TV, waiting for the solution to do its job and for any signs of movement. I think it took about an hour to take effect, and then I was trotting upstairs to the toilet. Bear in mind that what will be exiting your bowels is mostly not properly formed, so it is not like going to the toilet normally; it is more liquid.

It was then that I discovered that mixing the powder with fizzy water was probably not the best route to go down, as the gas from it exited at the same time, creating an explosion of gas and watery stools. I would not recommend it!

If possible, it is probably best that you are alone during this process or that the volume of the TV is turned up! Throughout the day, what I was passing became more and more liquid, until it was just like peeing out of my bottom. I was quite depressed at one point, as I was creating more pressure by peeing out of my bottom than out of my wiener!

While this process was going on, a smell was generated. That smell was the smell of my bowel, not like a normal smell after having gone to the toilet. It was a very distinctive smell, one that I found difficult to get rid of even with the window open. What I did discover was that a good squirt of bleach after each time I had been helped neutralise the odour. I found it far better than using a perfumed aerosol, as mixing the smell of lavender with it made it considerably worse!

During the night, I slept on an old towel and stuck some tissue paper between my cheeks just in case of leakage or I had an accident during the night, i.e., I thought I was going to break wind and more than gas came out! I walked around the day after with tissue still inserted, right up until I walked into the hospital. The insertion of tissue proved successful, as after my second colonoscopy, I thought I would go food shopping the next day. Halfway around the supermarket, I felt a rumbling down below, and before I could react, my bowel discharged itself! There was absolutely nothing I could do about it except abandon my trolley and make a dash for the doors!

When I went for my first colonoscopy, I was offered sedation during the procedure; there were various options available. I opted to take gas when I needed it, should it become too painful. Because I was having some form of sedation, my partner came with me and sat in the car reading a book in the hospital car park, as it wasn't advisable to drive home in such a condition, and I didn't want to be sat in the ward waiting for it to wear off if I had gone on my own; it is just not worth the risk.

I signed the consent form, basically saying that I understood what was going to be done to me and that I was aware that there were risks involved. There always are, aren't there? You even run the risk of side-effects from taking off-the-shelf painkillers. One of the risks in this case was bleeding. To ensure as quick a reaction as possible should anything go wrong, a cannula was inserted into a vein in my hand, allowing quick and easy access to my bloodstream should any medication or fluids need to be given.

The other risk is rupturing the colon's wall while performing the procedure. Not only could this cause bleeding, but it could also lead to the leakage of the contents of your bowel into the abdominal cavity. To access the colon, should either of these things take place, will probably require 'opening you up,' so if something goes wrong, it is not a quick, easy fix.

I got undressed, put my gown and socks on, and sat on my bed, waiting. It was really good actually, as they gave me a plastic container to put my belongings in, which was then put on my bed and came everywhere with me, so I wasn't worried about my phone, wallet, or any of my other belongings. The nurses were lovely and caring and made me comfortable before I was wheeled down the corridor, where I met the endoscopist who was going to carry out the procedure.

There were four or five people in the room with me altogether. How to use the gas was explained to me, and I was then asked to roll over onto my side into the foetal position so as to allow easy access to my bottom. The scope was inserted painlessly, thanks to some lubricant being applied, and I looked at the inside of my large colon on a screen. I found it fascinating. The inside of my colon was opaque in colour, with red lines criss-crossing it. The red lines turned out to be the blood supply to my colon.

The large colon is around five feet long and is responsible for 'mopping up' the remaining water and nutrients that the small colon hasn't, as well as absorbing vitamins and electrolytes and starting to form and solidify the remaining indigestible food into stools. Most of this happens in the ascending colon; the descending colon stores the stools, which are then transferred to the rectum by the contraction of the sigmoid colon; they are then ready to exit the body. The large colon is also responsible for creating certain vitamins from the trillions of bacteria living in it. There are four layers to the large colon, two of which are responsible for moving its contents along by way of contraction [6].

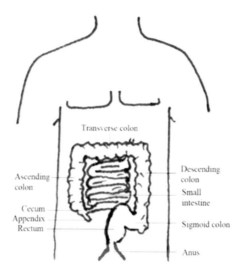

Diagram of the intestines

In relation to the large colon, the small colon is much longer (around twenty feet) and is responsible for extracting water and nutrients from our food [7]. It is important to understand the functions of the different parts of the large colon, as it may help you understand if you are having problems after surgery and why you are having those particular problems. I will explain and give an example later on.

As the colon is flexible, it can bend, twist, and compress; it is not like inserting a rod into a solid, straight tube. The endoscopist can twist and turn the scope as well as use air to inflate the colon where required to enable the scope's safe passage without damaging or perforating the colon. While all of this was going on, I was inhaling gas when I needed to. The pain I felt was similar to having bad stomach cramps. The cramps usually occurred during the inflation of the colon. Throughout the procedure, the nurses were reassuring me and telling me that I was doing well.

I watched the screen intently, silently praying that nothing that shouldn't be there showed up. The scope went up the descending colon, turned left along the transverse colon, and then turned down the ascending colon; everything was still okay. I thought that I was home and dry; in fact, the endoscopist congratulated me on how clean my colon was. The nurses told me not to worry, assuring me that only one in ten people ended up with something being found, and even then, it wasn't to say that what was found would be cancerous.

We got right to the very beginning of the ascending colon, where it meets the small intestine, and there it was, right at the end of the colonoscope's journey, a large polyp surrounded by a cloud of blood. When you compared it to the clean, opaque colour of the bowel, it was an angry red colour; it didn't look healthy.

A polyp is a growth usually caused by an abnormal growth

of cells and can be found in many areas of the body: on your skin, in the colon, in the ear, nose, and throat, etc. Most polyps are benign (not cancerous); some can turn into cancer, and some are cancerous [8].

My polyp was around forty millimetres wide! It was a large one. Polyps such as this are called flat polyps; they can stand on a stalk, making them look like mushrooms. This makes them harder to remove, as they can be close to the surface of the colon. When the endoscopist saw this, they took a biopsy for testing, and I was told that it was too large for them to remove and that a specialist in removing large polyps would have to carry out the operation.

A polyp in the colon is normally removed by an instrument that is part of the colonoscope. For a normal-sized polyp, a wire loop is extended out of the colonoscope and put around the polyp near its base. The wire is then tightened around the polyp and heated so that as the wire cuts through the polyp, the heat cauterises it and seals it, preventing blood loss and potential infection. How clever is that?

However, for a large flat polyp, the procedure is much more difficult, as you have to get the loop around a much larger mass, and the cauterising of the stalk is going to take place very close to the surface of the colon. There is also going to be more blood feeding the polyp; therefore, there will be a higher risk of blood loss.

When the procedure was over, I thanked everyone for their

care and for looking after me, and I went to get dressed. I messaged my partner that it was over and that I would meet her in the car park. When we met, I told her what had been found, and we embraced for a long time. We have been together for nearly thirty-two years and could not be without each other, so any risk to each other's health was very concerning and upsetting for us.

Not long after, I received a letter containing images that had been taken during the procedure using the scope, an explanation of what had been found, and the news that an appointment would be made to remove the polyp.

Meanwhile, I carried on with my life as normal, but with the thought of something inside of me that shouldn't be there and that had the potential to be life changing or even life ending. This is where I started to struggle, as I am a control freak. I have to be in control. Now I found myself in a position where I have no control. I was totally reliant on others, which didn't sit well with me.

It wasn't until five weeks later that I had my second colonoscopy. At least this time, I knew the procedure and what lay ahead. The only thing was that I had to go through the indignity of emptying my bowels again!

In preparation for my second colonoscopy, I did exactly the same again (stopped eating a day before I should have), but swapped the fizzy water for very cold still water when I mixed the laxative solution and held my breath while drinking it. This proved to be much better - not so bad a smell or taste.

I turned up at the hospital, leaving my partner ensconced in her car reading a book while I trotted off to the endoscopy department for a second time. I went through exactly the same procedure as before: I signed a consent form, got changed into my gown, and had a cannula attached to the top of my hand, which ended up being quite painful as it took four attempts to get the needle into a vein without going right through it! On the fourth attempt, I actually asked the nurse if it would be better if someone else did it!

The nurses were as pleasant as before, and I was duly wheeled down the corridor along with my belongings to the waiting endoscopist, who introduced himself. He turned out to be the senior consultant who was in charge of the unit. I was handed the gas mask, ready for when I needed it, and off we went again.

It was all pretty much the same as before, apart from being asked to move into various positions to enable the scope to make a safe passage through my colon. By changing position, it can affect pressure in various parts of the colon, and as the colon moves, it can allow passage of the scope. I learned this from the endoscopist and put it into practice when lying in bed after my operation. I will comment on this further in Chapter 4, The operation.

The scope went all the way down to the caecum again, and

this time I saw a different picture on the screen. I was mortified at the grizzly image that faced me. Why hadn't I seen this before during the initial inspection? Once it was in full view on the screen, everyone stopped, and a nurse put her hand on my shoulder.

It is only my supposition, but I am sure that the endoscopist was expecting to see something more than just a polyp when he got there. It is only my assumption, but I am thinking that it would be highly unlikely for a polyp of that size to be there on its own. I looked at what I saw in disbelief and asked, 'Is that it all around the edge?' The image was that of approximately two-thirds of the circumference of my colon being covered by the polyp and a growth.

This ugly mass bore the name caecal carcinoma. Due to them being found at the caecum (the furthest point of the large colon from your bottom), they can be difficult to detect due to their effects being slow to manifest themselves; therefore, there is the potential for them to grow to a large size before being detected [9].

After what seemed like a lifetime of silence, the endoscopist said that he would take a biopsy for analysis and that it was beyond just taking the polyp away. I was wheeled back to my room, got dressed, and had the cannula removed. One of the nurses called my partner on her mobile and asked if she could come and see me and the endoscopist.

The three of us sat down while what was found was

explained to my partner and I. We were told that I had a cancerous growth and that I could have surgery to remove it. I was given various pamphlets to take away with me and was told that the next stage of my treatment would be discussed at what is called an MDT meeting (Multi-Disciplinary Team meeting). These meetings usually took place at the end of each week.

Obviously, time can be critical with cancer, so now that I knew I definitely had it, I felt under pressure to get things moving, as two months had already passed from peeing blood to being told that I had cancer. It took two weeks to receive a call to tell me that I would be seen with a view to having an operation. That operation would turn out to be a laparoscopic right hemicolectomy!

2

My thoughts and actions having been diagnosed

After meeting my consultant, I received a letter confirming the stage and state of the cancer: I had a caecal adenocarcinoma (cancer of the caecum) T2 N0 M0. Let me explain:

T2 indicates that the muscle layer of the bowel wall has been invaded by the tumour.
N0 indicates that cancer cells have not been found in any nearby lymph nodes.
M0 indicates that there has been no spread of cancer to other parts of the body [10].

The lymph system is a network similar to veins that carry blood around the body; instead of carrying blood, lymph vessels carry lymph, a clear fluid that contains white blood cells. The lymph system helps fight infection by capturing and storing foreign substances in lymph nodes. Cancer cells, germs, and infections can be destroyed by immune cells contained within the nodes. There are lymph nodes around the bowel area [11].

Although cancer cells can be killed off in lymph nodes, some may escape and start to form a tumour in a different part of the body; this is called metastasis (M) [12].

If cancer cells escape and are not killed by your body, they can travel through your lymph system and bloodstream to other parts of your body, as well as invade tissue close to their origin to then create a tumour, although in some instances it can be years before the cells start to develop further. Interestingly, even if it has spread elsewhere, it is still called by its original name, but with metastatic put in front of it, e.g., metastatic colon cancer. It can also be called stage 4 (IV) cancer, depending on the type of cancer. With regards to colon cancer, the usual sites where it spreads to are the lungs, liver, and peritoneum [13].

The peritoneum lines your abdominal cavity and covers your abdominal organs. Invading the peritoneum makes sense, as your large colon is right next to it and comes into contact with it, like mine did; it showed signs of adhesion to the abdominal wall. If my cancer had grown through the outer wall of my colon, then it could have come into direct contact with the peritoneum, which I would assume would have made the spread of cancer much easier and quicker.

As per the bowel, it is important to keep your immune system healthy; therefore, it is not surprising that the same things that are mentioned in Chapter 12 (Colon cancer and what causes it) that help to maintain a healthy body are the same as those required to maintain a healthy immune system.

It seems that every time we diverge from our natural state, we put ourselves at risk, and the more we diverge, the more risk we put ourselves at.

When I was told that I had the disease, it came as something of a shock, which is putting it mildly. Very soon, my shock turned to anger - anger at myself - as I felt that my body had let me down; it had failed me. I felt as though I was standing on the edge of an abyss. I also felt very alone, even though I had the love and support of my long-term, loving partner.

It is a strange feeling to be told that you have a disease that could kill you. You might think I felt alone because I chose not to tell anyone. It is difficult to explain: I was the one that had it; those around me didn't; therefore, I was the odd one out.

I immediately started searching for information relating to patient mortality; what was my life expectancy? Having read countless articles and having spoken to people, I decided not to be governed by it and didn't include it in my writing.

Calculations and outcomes relating to life expectancy can be dependent upon so many factors, such as what type of cancer it is, how advanced the cancer is, your age, your general state of health, if you have any existing comorbidities, how you react to treatment, treatments that are available to you, timelines, and then there is the factor of luck or bad luck. In my mind, your consultant and medical team will be the best people to discuss this topic with.

So now I am in the 'one in two people in the UK who will develop cancer in their lifetime' category. To start with, I could hardly say the word cancer because my mind was filled with all of the negative connotations relating to it, primarily a long-lasting, painful illness and subsequent death. I hated the word; it made me so angry and resentful. Perhaps if I hadn't already been witness to the aftermath of it, having known people who had it and are no longer here, I wouldn't have felt so bad, but I had, and I did.

I have experienced two of my friends' fathers, a school friend, as well as my partner's father dying from it. Friends and acquaintances have also had some form of it. I am pleased to say that more, rather than less, are still around to tell the tale, which shows how far treatment of this disease has come.

I am using the word disease to cover all cancers, as there are so many. They all have their own treatments and specialists. We will look at this later in the book, in Chapter 11 - Cancer in general.

To me, getting cancer was something that happened to other people, not to me. I was in my mid-to-late fifties, I was fit and healthy (at least I thought I was), and I was banking on having another fifteen to twenty good years ahead of me. My partner and I had our future planned out; it was all sorted. I had retired early and had accumulated pensions and savings to see the two of us through to our dotage.

I remember talking to a couple of customers in relation to retirement (we were all around the same age), and they both said that we probably have another fifteen good years left in us. We all looked at each other and said, 'It's not long, is it?' This really affirmed my thoughts about retiring while I was still young and fit enough to enjoy myself. Funnily enough, cancer hadn't entered my mind at that point, but why should it have, as I didn't drink alcohol, had never smoked, didn't take drugs, wasn't overweight, and going to see my GP was a rarity?

While walking along the coast with my partner, we often saw old couples sitting together or meandering along holding hands and would say, 'That will be us one day.' Everything had been planned; how dare something come along and try to ruin our hard fought for future? I am afraid that is what it does; it has no compassion; it doesn't take into account your plans or the fact that the two of us couldn't bear to be without each other; it can be completely and utterly indiscriminate, shows no feelings or remorse, and has no moral compass.

Having said that, I feel that I have achieved what I set out to achieve, and that was to keep my partner safe and well provided for both now and for the rest of her life; however, if my health does go pear-shaped, then I feel that I will have failed, as we had planned to be together into our dotage; I simply cannot bear to think of her being on her own.

Even though I had been diagnosed with it, I still hadn't told anyone yet - not family or friends. I am a very private person; this, coupled with my need to be in control, prevented me from communicating what was happening to me to others until I had gotten a handle on what was going on myself. I could not cope with my phone constantly 'pinging' as it received messages asking if I was okay or what was going to happen next. I didn't even know myself at that point. I needed to understand it more, along with the possible outcomes, before I started communicating with people about it.

However, there was one person in whom I did confide. I saw a friend who was separate from my other friends not long after being diagnosed, and they asked me how I was. I looked at them, trying not to burst into tears, and told them. To my astonishment, they said that they were also being checked for cancer. We both laughed an incredulous laugh. How bizarre!

We had both been through two invasive procedures (a cystoscopy and a colonoscopy), along with ultrasound scans, and whereas mine was confirmed, theirs was still being investigated. In the end, they were found to have a polyp in their colon, which was removed and treated by radiotherapy. They were also thought to have diverticulitis, which in the end was confirmed as IBS (irritable bowel syndrome). The difference between us was that they'd had obvious symptoms (pain in the abdomen, stomach cramps, etc.), whereas I hadn't.

From then on, we kept in touch to see how each other was progressing and to support each other. As I am not a social media or group forum person, having someone that I trusted and knew to speak to was a huge help. I hope it was the same for them too.

What made matters worse was that my mother has dementia, and so there was little point in telling her or upsetting her should she have understood what I was saying. She was also partly deaf, so you had to raise your voice for her to hear you. You can imagine me in the care home shouting, 'Mum, I have some bad news - I have cancer. I have cancer, mum. Cancer. Oh, forget it!' This, while everyone was having a good earwig! Later on, friends did ask whether I had told mum; I explained that I had not and why.

Due to the care home having had outbreaks of COVID, I wasn't that keen on going, bearing in mind my condition and the importance of not catching COVID; therefore, I explained my position to the carers so that they didn't think that I had abandoned her. I certainly didn't want them calling to tell me that mum was asking why I hadn't been to see her. You do have to think about everyone around you and how best to deal with the situation, as it affects them too.

One thing that I said to my partner was that she was to speak to whoever she needed to so that she could vent her feelings, as long as they were people that I didn't communicate with. She spoke to her employers, colleagues, and friends at work, along with her own circle of friends. What I didn't want to happen was that she bottled it all up; that would have been grossly unfair. Yes, we obviously spoke about what was going on, but she will speak differently to her friends in a way that she cannot speak to me.

My mind soon started to think about the worst-case scenario:

passing away. In my own personal experience, it had always been the fathers that had passed away - the men. I started to think about not being around anymore. It was hard to get my head around. My first thoughts were for my partner; I just could not let her be left alone on her own. This thought drove me forward: I had to stay alive for her; otherwise, I would have failed.

To hopefully help her should the worst happen, I even planned to buy both birthday and Christmas presents until she was in her seventies. I figured out the type of things that I would be able to buy for her (her clothes size, I assume, would change as she got older), along with where to hide them. I thought it would be nice to keep getting something from me to say that I was still there for her. I even thought of recording a short video to go along with each present. You are probably thinking that I am a bit crazy. You would not be the first!

We both had wills in place, so that was okay. Financially, we were in a very favourable position, so that wasn't a problem either, although I did think about transferring the house and all of my financial assets over to her so that it would make life easier for her. I thought about my funeral, the music that I wanted playing, and even whether I should record some goodbye messages for my friends and people that I loved. I suppose I just wanted them to know how much I loved them and what they meant to me. As days pass into years, the opportunities to say how you feel about someone can pass you by, and then it can be too late.

For years, I joked that I would be the first one to go and that my partner could then get a dog and her own horse; she wouldn't need to work, and she would be too busy riding her horse or playing with her pooch to miss me. I also joked with my mother that she would outlive me. I wish that I had kept my mouth shut, as these outcomes were now staring me starkly in the face!

My arrogance led me to ask forgiveness from a friend due to my going on about not wanting to be a burden to my partner should I become ill. It had more to do with my mother's illness than anything else - the thought of losing your faculties and the burden that was imposed on your partner. One thing that all of this led my partner and I to discuss was sorting out a power of attorney for each other. It makes more logical sense the older you get.

I used to say, 'If I was losing my mind, I would pop some tablets, wave goodbye, and I would be on my way.' However, when I was faced with it, all I wanted to do was be there for my partner; the thought of leaving her on her own to deal with the aftermath and the loneliness was unbearable. I would fight to the very end to spend more time with her because I love her so much.

Now I have tears rolling down my face! Mind you, I cry while watching the new Paddington movies, so it is no surprise. While I am typing, postie has arrived. On opening the mail, the first envelope contained details relating to saving for your funeral. Thanks, postie, I needed that - not!

Once the melancholy started to wear off, one of the first things that I thought about was, how did I get it? I have never smoked, although my parents made me a passive smoker for fourteen years, which still makes me angry, as does seeing someone puffing on one, especially outside a hospital; I didn't think that my family had a history of cancer (now thinking about it, I think that my grandfather on my mother's side died of stomach or bowel cancer when he was in his seventies); I drank alcohol as a typical teenager does, but stopped in my early twenties as my job entailed a lot of driving; my diet was reasonable apart from lots of chocolate (I have a very sweet tooth); and I ate red meat as well as processed meat, but I wouldn't say copious amounts of them.

So how and why did I get it? It could be simple bad luck - nothing more, nothing less. I could have spent days beating myself up trying to understand how and why I got it, but I will never know.

We will look at what cancer is, what can cause it, and what treatments there are, along with new developments in relation to bowel cancer and other cancers, later in the book.

All of this happened during the COVID-19 pandemic, when the NHS was being stretched to breaking point; therefore, every visit to the hospital entailed having to go there a few days before to have a swab taken. An obvious concern to me was catching COVID, as I would not be allowed into the hospital, which would mean further delays in relation to tests or the operation itself, and the clock was already ticking.

My partner and I both became very aware of the ramifications should either of us catch COVID; it simply meant that we just could not afford to catch it. Every time I went into the hospital, I took sanitiser, wore gloves, and wore two masks - not just for my sake but for everyone's sake. My partner was also very careful; we both were.

One of my next thoughts was - would I be better off going private? I asked myself this question for two reasons: 1) I am a private person and would struggle being in a ward with lots of other people, and 2) would I be able to have my operation quicker if I went private?

With this in mind, I turned the computer on and started searching for private hospitals and colon cancer. I read about the aftercare that was offered along with the various post-operative treatments that were available, such as radiotherapy and chemotherapy. Local hospitals were searched first, and I was soon on the phone to find out what was available and what kind of cost was involved.

The response was somewhat disappointing, as they told me that due to the pandemic, they didn't have sufficient theatre staff to perform the operations that they currently had booked, let alone new ones. They advised me to stay with the NHS, as I was already well down the path of my diagnosis and planned treatment. This hit home how bad the situation was in relation to COVID affecting healthcare and hospitals. Whether nurses, consultants, or surgeons are private or NHS, if there aren't enough of them, then it doesn't matter which side they are on.

When I started searching, I also looked at individual surgeons and consultants, only to find that the majority of them worked for both the NHS and in private hospitals. I was going to look further afield, but my partner was conscious of being away from me should anything happen; therefore, I decided to stick with the NHS and kept my fingers crossed for a reasonably quick date.

Throughout the book, I comment on the NHS, what they have done for me, and how they have done it. Are they perfect? No, they are not. Am I perfect? I most certainly am not. Were they there for me when I was in need of help? Yes, they were.

The NHS has been allowed to turn into a leviathan and needs help; of that, there is no doubt. I know one thing: I couldn't do their job, whether it be a porter, a nurse, or a GP. You really have to be a caring person with a lot of empathy for whoever walks through that door - a people person - and I admit that I could not be that person, not for anyone or everyone, not unless that person is a loved one or is close to me. My persona is very much all or nothing; therefore, I would struggle dealing with strangers.

One thing that I do know is that I owe my life to them, however long that may be, and I will be forever grateful for the care and empathy shown to me during my treatments. Thank you all.

3

The lead up to my operation

Now things have started to happen. I had been given a date to see a consultant. Letters started arriving thick and fast relating to more blood tests, a CT scan, as well as pre-assessment calls and meetings prior to the operation. Even though they were four to six weeks away, it gave me a boost. I now had dates to put in my diary, which gave me something to look forward to and be positive about.

My first port of call was to meet a consultant in a hospital around thirty miles away. My partner came with me, and we double-masked, and I wore disposable gloves too. The letter said that I would most likely be examined, so I wore clothes that were easy to take off and put back on again.

We arrived early and were ushered through to meet the consultant, who was accompanied by a sister who was a part of the colorectal nurse team. The consultant made us feel at ease by asking me questions about what I did, my health, my level of fitness, if I was on any medication, if I had any symptoms, and whether I drank alcohol or smoked, and then began to explain the benefits of having my operation at that particular hospital.

The designated hospital operated as a COVID-free hospital, meaning that it did not accept COVID patients for treatment. The benefit from this was that the date that I was given for my operation would most likely remain the same, unlike my local hospital, which accepted COVID patients, meaning that my date could be put back and put back depending upon how many COVID admissions there were.

I asked if they wanted to examine me - did they want me to get undressed? The response was a resounding 'no,' which surprised me. The consultant offered me a file and asked if there was anything missing, to which I gave a puzzled look.

The point being made was that there was just one page in my medical file. I was told that they usually get files that are inches thick. I responded that I wasn't a hospital person, in that the only times that I had been in a hospital were when I got knocked off my motorcycle as a teenager. I was told that I was a prime candidate for having my operation at that hospital due to my health, high level of fitness, good BMI (body mass index), weight, lack of allergies, and the fact that I wasn't diabetic or obese and was on no medication. I was told unfalteringly, 'You are coming here.'

I can only think that the page related to an incident a couple of years ago, on the evening of Christmas Eve. In the evening, I started to experience pain in my stomach or abdomen. The pain wasn't constant; it started off low and then kept on increasing until I was doubled up on the floor, and then it would go back down again. I had a couple of minutes break before it started again; it was cyclical – it kept on repeating itself.

My partner drove me to A&E, where I nearly passed out in

front of the receptionist. Thankfully, a couple of nurses nearby caught me and took me into a room to get me sat down. As I sat down, I realised that my t-shirt was soaking wet with sweat. I should not have been sweating in late December!

Within minutes, a cannula was fitted, and a blood sample was taken for analysis. It was after this that I was introduced to morphine. Oh, what joy! I remember saying to my partner, 'I understand why people steal it now,' laughing as I did so. Six hours later and another shot of morphine, the pain had gone and my abdomen wasn't swollen anymore. I never did get an answer as to what happened. There was conjecture that it could have been a gallstone passing through. All I know is that it hurt like hell.

The reason why I could have my operation at that particular hospital was that, due to the above positives and not foregoing any major problems during surgery, I should not need intensive care. This was important because they didn't have an ICU (intensive care unit). If there was an unforeseen problem during the operation, I would have to be stabilised and transferred to an ambulance, which would then travel post-haste the thirty miles to my local hospital.

The interesting thing relating to my discussion with a certain private hospital group was that they didn't have an ICU either, nor did they have surgeons available during the night. With such a complicated surgery and the very bad ramifications should there be a leak or an infection, going private did not sit that comfortably with me. In fact, the NHS looked more and more appealing!

What my appointed hospital did have was something called HDUs (high dependency units). These were halfway houses between intensive care and a normal ward. An HDU is for people who need intensive monitoring and care and usually has a slightly higher number of staff than a normal ward. This is where I would be placed after my operation.

Bearing in mind the mention of intensive care, I asked what could go wrong during the operation and was told there could be a number of things, such as bleeding, the need for a stoma, infections of the chest and wounds, as well as internal infections, which could lead to sepsis.

Sepsis is extremely dangerous. Sepsis can be caused by an extreme body reaction to an infection, which can lead to death. The gastrointestinal tract is one of the areas where infections, which can lead to sepsis, most commonly start [14]!

I asked the consultant what having a stoma meant. The reply was that if there are complications during the surgery and the bowel needs time to heal before it is reconnected, then a stoma may be created as a temporary fix to allow things to heal properly.

Basically, a stoma is an opening made in the abdominal wall to which the colon is attached. A stoma bag is then attached to collect your body waste from the bowel. This operation can be reversed by way of a second operation once what has been given time to heal has healed, allowing the bowel to be reconnected. However, sometimes the stoma can be permanent [15]. This worried me greatly.

After it was explained to me, I said, 'I can't; I just can't. I ride horses and compete in dressage; I can't have something sticking out of me as I wear tight-fitting clothes for riding. I just can't.' I was told that other people have had stomas fitted and they still go swimming, and some of them ride horses. I repeated myself again: 'I can't have one; it would be the end of me. I don't think that I could live with one.'

The consultant told me that their job was to get rid of the cancer, and that is exactly what they will do by cutting a section of my colon out. During the operation, I will obviously be under anaesthesia, so I will know nothing about what is going on.

If the surgeon came across problems, then obviously they couldn't discuss them with me; they had to act there and then. I was told that due to my level of fitness, it would be highly unlikely that there would be a problem, but nevertheless, they must discuss a stoma with me as it might need to be done whether I liked it or not.

I then threw a spanner in the works by asking, 'What would happen if I didn't have it?' Judging from the answer, my question had been misunderstood, so I asked, 'What if I don't have the operation at all?' which came as a surprise to everyone but me. I was told that if I didn't have the operation, the tumour would grow; it would most likely lead to a blockage of the intestine, which would mean surgery anyway; I would almost definitely end up with a stoma; and it would most likely start to spread to other parts of my body.

Basically, it would be game over; I really did not have a choice if I was to stand a chance of surviving it. At this point, my partner was in tears.

We then moved onto the hospital itself, and I admitted that I had looked into going private and that it was no disrespect to those people in the room or the NHS in general. I explained that I am a private person and that my recovery would be faster if I was able to have peace and quiet. Not having been in a hospital ward since my late teens, my concept of a ward was a dozen beds down each side with one toilet between everyone and having to put up with people trying to make small talk and the coughing, groaning, and wheezing that takes place during the night.

It was brought to my attention that modern-day wards are now usually made up of bays, with each bay having between four and six beds. I repeated my need for privacy and asked if there was a possibility of having my own room for the reasons already stated. I offered to pay £300 or £500 a night, as I was going to have to pay if I went private anyway. If the nightly payment wasn't possible, I offered to make a sizeable donation to the hospital.

I was told that the problem with putting me in a single room was down to staffing again. The reason being that the single beds were located away from the bays; therefore, a nurse would have to keep leaving the bays to see just one person, and due to the type of surgery that I was having, there would need to be regular visits. If they were short-staffed one night, then it would cause them a real problem. At this point, I still didn't really understand how major an operation I was going to have.

The surgery that I was going to have is called a laparoscopic right hemicolectomy (it is a mouthful, isn't it?), which is where the right-hand side of the colon is removed along with a small section of the small colon where it joins the large colon. The caecum is at this joint, so this is also removed [16]. Laparoscopy basically means keyhole surgery.

There are two ways of entering the abdomen or pelvic area; the simplest is by way of a large incision that allows the surgeon to open the abdomen up, giving them plenty of room and visibility to carry out the operation. The advantage of this 'open' surgery is that it is quicker than keyhole surgery and easier for the surgeon. The downside for the patient is that their recovery takes longer due to a much larger incision having been made (usually meaning a longer stay in the hospital), more scarring, and probably more pain and bleeding.

To enable the surgeon and their team to carry out keyhole surgery, a laparoscope is used. This slimline tube includes a light and a video camera, which are linked to a monitor, enabling everyone to see what they are doing. Several small incisions are made to allow the insertion of the laparoscope, an air line, and any instruments being used during the operation. A tube linked to a supply of carbon dioxide is inserted into one of the incisions, enabling the abdomen to be expanded so as to give the team more room to manoeuvre and better visibility. Once inflated, the laparoscope can be inserted. The other incisions are there for small surgical instruments to be used during the procedure, and a larger incision is there for taking the bowel out. Once the operation has been completed, the incisions are usually stitched back up using dissolvable stitches, and dressings are applied [17].

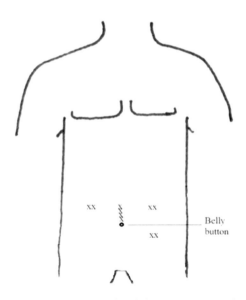

xxx - where my incisions were made.

My keyhole surgery involved three small incisions, which were about two centimetres wide, and a larger incision, which was around six centimetres long. The larger incision was directly above my belly button. To be honest, they never really caused me any problems – they didn't hurt, didn't bleed, didn't really cause me any discomfort, and didn't become infected; they healed really well. Fourteen months later, they are barely visible. I look at them and can now imagine what was happening during the operation and the apparatuses that were being used.

After discussing the operation, I asked how the large colon and the small colon were attached to each other, as I understood one had a larger diameter than the other. I was told that even though they are called small and large, they are in fact quite similar in size, so it is not a problem. I then asked how they were attached to each other during the operation and how they could be attached so that they would not leak - staples, stitching? 'Very good stitching,' was the reply.

If the stitching leaked after I had been stapled back up again, it could be very bad for me - maybe weeks in the hospital due to infection, another operation, and the potential creation of a stoma. I really did not want a leak!

I struggled to comprehend how this intricate surgery could be done by keyhole, if it could be done at all, especially stitching the large and small colon together without leaking. It is at this point that you thank God that there are people who are interested in this part of the anatomy because, let's face it, it is not the most glamorous, is it? I know that there is no way I could deal with someone else's rectal problems. I take my hat off to them and thank them from the bottom of my heart, because without them, I and many others would not be here.

During the operation, I knew that I would be anaesthetised. I wanted to discuss pain relief after the operation, as one of the colorectal nurses had mentioned it to me. The normal method is epidural, which is the insertion of a catheter near the nerves in your spine, allowing pain relief medication to be administered through the catheter. The medicine numbs your chest, abdomen, and legs; this form of pain relief is commonly used in childbirth.

I did not want any needles or injections anywhere near my spine. It comes back to the need to be in control again. If I woke up unable to feel parts of my body, I would freak out.

When I was a teenager, while riding a motorcycle, I was hit head-on by a car. This culminated in me being propelled straight through the car's windscreen. As my helmet impacted the windscreen, I vividly remember the sensation of my spine and neck compressing as the weight of my body still travelled forward even though my head had stopped. Thankfully, the pressure on my spine and neck released as the windscreen shattered and I travelled through it.

To make matters worse, my passenger travelled over the top of me, bounced off the roof, and squashed me between the roof and the steering wheel. It was so bad that I had to be cut free by the fire brigade; they literally cut the roof of the car off. The one thing that I remember, apart from spitting glass out of my mouth and screaming blue murder when I came around, was not feeling my legs. I have never been so frightened in my life.

This could have been due to two things: the numbing of my legs as they smashed against the bonnet of the car or the compression of my spine. To extricate me, two members of the fire crew formed a cradle with their arms and carried me away from the car while I screamed, 'I can't feel my legs.' Funnily enough, I never want to not feel my legs again!

With this in mind, we discussed self-medication rather than an epidural. This is when you have a form of pain relief, say morphine, for instance, that you can self-administer by just pressing a button. It is really simple; when you need pain relief, you just press a button, and the drug is administered by a pump intravenously straight into a vein straight into your bloodstream. You cannot overdose, as the equipment will only allow a certain number of set doses per hour. This seemed ideal for me, and we agreed that this would be the way forward rather than having an epidural.

Having answered all of my questions, I apologised and explained why I needed to know what was going to happen, along with the whys and wherefores. Having been in control of various companies and their operations, I knew everything that was going on and calculated every decision that I made to ensure the best possible outcome. I was in charge; I was in control, and I was happiest in this position. I had no previous knowledge of the disease that I was now told I had, and so to make myself more at ease with the situation, I needed to understand it.

We wrapped up the meeting by me asking the consultant the same question that I asked my pension advisor, and that was, 'Will you look after me?' I have dealt with people all through my career, and when I ask a person an important question while looking them in the eye, I know whether I can trust them or not. I am pleased to say that in this instance, as per my pension advisor, I felt in very safe hands and could therefore relax and let them get on with it.

When there are important decisions to be made that involve other people, I like to try and make a connection with them so that they know me a bit better, understand where I am coming from, how important this decision is to me, and that I am not just another customer or number. I was pleased that I had made this particular connection.

Just before I left, a prescription was given to me to collect from the hospital pharmacy. We duly went to the pharmacy and walked away with a carrier bag full of medicines and syringes. It was literally a carrier bag full! Both the consultant and the sister were lovely, and I will be forever grateful to them and their team. Thank you.

As well as the individual meetings, I was given various

phone numbers relating to the colorectal nurse team, which covered a number of hospitals. They specialise in colorectal patients only, providing support and answers to any questions that you may have. It was nice to know that if something was niggling me or if something had changed physically, then I had a direct line to people who counted - people who knew my history and disposition.

I was also told that I would be on a five-year plan, where I would be monitored by way of blood tests, colonoscopies, phone calls, and scans, and that I would always have the colorectal nurses as a direct point of contact.

After my meeting with the consultant, I started to get a barrage of appointments. One of the most important letters was the confirmation of my operation. This was five weeks away. In total, it will have been nearly five months since I first peed blood, and even though things were starting to happen and I had a date, I was still worried about my cancer spreading.

It was sod's law that we had our holiday booked at this same time. I was happy that this was to be the only glitch, not a puncture or the car breaking down on the way to the hospital. Obviously, there was no hesitation in carrying on with the operation at the appointed date. I called the hotel and explained our position, and they were very kind. We rescheduled for the coming year, which gave us something to look forward to.

The next step was going to the hospital for my second blood sample. There are various things that a blood sample can tell you: whether there are cancer cells in your blood, if there are other cells in your blood that have been created by cancer, such as proteins, and if your organs are functioning properly. The different types of blood cells are counted during a complete blood count (blood cancers can be detected during this); certain proteins are looked for, which can in turn help highlight a type of bone marrow cancer; and chemicals given off by cancers are looked for during a tumour marker test; for instance, CEA (carcinoembryonic antigen) is relevant to colon cancer; CA 125 (cancer antigen 125) is relevant to ovarian cancer; PSA (prostate-specific antigen) is relevant to prostate cancer, and alpha-fetoprotein is relevant to testicular cancer [18].

The CEA marker can vary depending on whether you are male, female, or a smoker. For instance, the median number for a male would be 3.4, compared to a female's 2.5. If you are a smoker, the male median number would be 6.2, as opposed to 4.9 for a female. Increased CEA numbers are not only attributed to cancer but can also point towards other gastrointestinal diseases [19].

Other tests that can be carried out on your blood samples include looking for genetic material (DNA) that may have come away from cancer cells as they grow and die, as well as looking for circulating tumour cells (cells that have come away from their origin and are circulating around your body) [20].

I remember during my partner's father's illness, the word 'marker' kept being used. Markers are not the be-all and end-all with respect to a cancer diagnosis, as many healthy cells and certain other conditions can also give off these markers.

A lot of the time, markers are monitored post-procedure to see if what has been done has made a difference [21].

The benefit of taking readings beforehand is that it gives a baseline for future readings to be compared to: are the readings increasing, decreasing, or staying the same compared to pre-procedure? A blood test is not a test to be used on its own but is part of a package of tests that helps determine your prognosis.

Next on the agenda, just two days after my blood test, was a CT scan, which I had never had before.

A CT scan consists of lying still on a bed that moves in and out of a ring-shaped scanner. The scanner takes multiple images (x-rays), the information of which is transferred to a series of cross-sectional images, which are collated to produce a 3D image of the area in question. It can take images of many parts of the body, such as the pelvis, spine, brain, chest, and abdomen [22]. If you are having treatment for cancer, by taking a scan before and after treatment, you can see what effect the treatment is actually having.

As with any procedure, there is risk. The risk of developing cancer due to the radiation from the x-rays is said to be very small, even if you have lots of CT scans. There is also a small risk of having an allergic reaction to the dye, should you be given it. The risks of having a scan will be discussed with you [23].

When I had mine, it took around twenty-five minutes from start to finish. I had to have a cannula put in my arm to allow dye to be injected into my bloodstream; dye intensifies the quality of the images. I didn't find it painful or worrisome. I had a warm feeling as it travelled through my veins and around my body, as well as a metallic taste in my mouth. It was an odd feeling. I was told to drink plenty of water afterwards to help flush the dye out. In answer to what you may be thinking, no, my pee did not come out purple or any other strange colour.

The next day, I had a pre-assessment call to discuss what was going to happen, where I needed to go, and any preparation that I might need to do beforehand. I had never been to the hospital so much, apart from taking my mum when she was in the early stages of dementia.

Around this time, we had theatre tickets booked to see a comedian. With COVID still prevalent, we decided that the risk was not worth taking and gave them to friends. It was a shame, as we both could have done with a giggle.

Just under a week later, I was at the hospital again for my pre-assessment checks and discussions. All of these checks were taking place at my local hospital; I was not travelling thirty miles each time.

My first port of call was simple: a check of my blood pressure. I hated blood pressure checks because, as soon as I felt the band being strapped on, I could feel myself tightening up and stressing. They are not painful; it was just the thought that my readings would lead to something else. My blood pressure was said to be high, as it was when I had my blood samples taken at my GP. I always knew that I would end up with high blood pressure due to the nature of my work and the pressure I put myself under.

Working twelve to sixteen hour days for years whilst under a lot of pressure was bound to take its toll. My mum also has high blood pressure. I can remember taking her to the hospital for a check-up, and they took her blood pressure. I watched the screen as it settled over two hundred! I said, 'Bloody hell, you should be dead with a reading like that.' It was probably not the right thing to say under the circumstances!

My readings were coming out at around 175/116, which wasn't good. The nurse told me that I needed to get it under control; otherwise, there is a chance that they may not operate. This certainly did not help my demeanour. I then went on to have an ECG (electrocardiogram), which checks your heart's electrical signals and its rhythm. I was asked if I had heart palpitations, which I admitted to; they were only occasional, though. It is a strange feeling, as my heart seems to bounce about a bit as though it is readjusting itself. It then settles back down again. No problems were picked up during this test.

After having an ECG, I went to meet some anaesthetists who were going to explain about having an anaesthetic during my operation. It was an amusing meeting, as the topic seemed to revolve around the odds of dying during the operation. The purpose of an anaesthetic was explained to me, and I quickly steered the conversation onto post-operation pain relief and the method of administration that I had agreed with the consultant. This seemed to be accepted without a problem, which then led us to the odds of me making it through the operation.

Having reviewed my medical data, taking into account my BMI, weight, height, etc., I was told that I had a one in three hundred chance of dying on the operating table. One in three hundred! This worked out to a 0.3% chance of dying. I could not believe it. I was expecting a one in two thousand or more chance, not a one in three hundred chance. I was then asked if I still wanted to proceed. I laughed and said, 'Well, I haven't got much choice, have I?'

In fact, I had no choice because if I didn't have the operation, the cancer would spread and kill me. Not having the operation carries a risk rate of 100%! They both nodded in agreement, and I went on my way. So, the next time I would see a hospital was in nine days' time.

Due to COVID and my operation being so close, my partner

and I decided it was best to self-isolate at home ten days before my operation. If I caught COVID, I would lose my slot; it is not as though they can sit around waiting for me, and it could be weeks or even months before I got another date.

Self-isolation was mentally punishing for both of us. My partner would come home and go straight upstairs and into the main bedroom. I would cook tea and take it up to her with a drink, and after we had eaten, we would sit on the landing fifteen feet apart, talking about each other's day. She would then close the door when we had finished talking. I took her plate away and would then wash up and watch TV in the lounge while she read or watched TV in the bedroom. When it was late enough, we would both say goodnight, and I would go to the second bedroom, where I would be sleeping for the duration.

You would not think it would be so difficult, would you? We had a bedroom each and were still talking and seeing each other. The hard part was not being able to have any physical contact - to hold each other, to have a hug. We are both very tactile in that way; we are always holding hands or snuggling up on the sofa, so to have no contact at all was really difficult.

We would sit, one at each end of the landing, in tears. It was made all the worse due to the reason why we were isolating: I had to have a major operation to remove a tumour, which is upsetting enough in itself.

A couple of months before the operation, I had a puncture, and that worried me in relation to travelling to the hospital. The journey took around forty minutes, and at the time we were travelling, there wouldn't be that many people about; I had to be at the hospital for seven thirty in the morning. I duly called some local taxi firms, both where I live and where I was going. I needed a backup plan in case something went wrong. Let's face it, if something is going to happen, it usually happens when you really don't want it to.

I contacted the friend who I mentioned earlier, explained my worry, and asked if they would travel behind us so that if anything went wrong, they could pick me up and carry on taking me to the hospital. They agreed, which was a great relief to me. All bases were covered!

Days passed by, and a week before the operation, I started to run through my medication. The list that I had been given was in alphabetical order, which was useless in relation to when the different medicines needed to be taken. I made my own list based on the times that they needed to be taken and the dose that needed to be taken.

I had a carrier bag full of high calorie drinks, a high protein powder mix, more dreaded laxatives, copious amounts of antibiotics, and a syringe to inject myself with an anti-blood clotting medicine (commonly known as a blood thinner or an anticoagulant). I have never injected myself before, so I was a little worried about it.

I started packing a bag ready for my stay, as I wasn't sure what they had at the hospital or how long I was going to be there, so I probably took more than I needed - better to be safe than sorry, I thought. Biscuits, boiled sweets, squash, books, a puzzle magazine, t-shirts, shorts, underwear, socks, shampoo, body wash, wet wipes, a mobile phone and charger, a small amount of cash, my glasses, a baseball cap, slippers, and a towel should just about do it! I didn't want to get there and find that I was missing something.

One of the colorectal nurses called me to touch base and make sure that I was prepared for my surgery. I asked about extending the period of not eating before I took the laxatives, as I had done for my colonoscopies. I was told in no uncertain terms that I must not do this and that I must eat the day before as per the instructions. It was only then that it hit home how much pressure my body was going to be put under during the operation, as the nurse explained what my body was going to have to cope with whilst I was anaesthetised.

Throughout surgery, your body is put through great stress and trauma. You will know nothing about it, as you will be out for the count, oblivious to what is going on. If you think about it logically, what is your body going to do if it feels like it is under attack as it is being cut open, bleeding, sensing pain, having parts removed, and being stitched or stapled? It will react accordingly to the messages sent from the nervous system. The body will be doing everything it can to try to contain and heal what is happening to it. The body will be in overdrive.

If your surgery lasts eight hours or so, that is an awful long time for your body to be fighting to protect and maintain itself. During this period, your body will be consuming vast amounts of energy; this is where the high calorie and high protein drinks come in, and this is why I was told that I must eat as per the instructions. If I had not eaten, I would have deprived my body of the vital calories it required for the operation. I did as I was told and ate my scrambled eggs on toast and cheese sandwiches using white bread.

I had no appreciation for how important it was to be fit and healthy until this happened, but then again, I had not planned to have such a major operation. I was very pleased that I was in good physical order; otherwise, I could have had a much harder ride.

Two days before the operation, I started medicating. The day before was the worst, as every hour I was taking something until around ten o'clock at night. I finished packing my bag according to what I thought I needed, which turned out to be far too much, and waited for tomorrow to arrive.

On the day of surgery, our alarm went off at half past five in the morning, and I took my final medication. We left the house and saw my friend parked around the corner, who duly followed a discreet distance behind us. I will always be grateful for their help and support during what was a dark and difficult time. I hope that I supported them as much.

We arrived at the hospital in good time, and we held each

other for some time before I bid my farewell and walked through the doors.

4

The operation

When I started to put a timeline together for things that occurred during my stay, I could not believe how so much had happened to me in such a short period of time. I always remember looking back on certain aspects and thinking, it can't have happened that quick. It was but a blur!

Day 1
Well, there I was, in the hospital. As soon as I entered the ward, I was made to feel at home, and a specific nurse was assigned to me to sort me out. I was tagged to ensure that I was who I said I was and that I wouldn't wake up without an arm or a leg due to being mistaken for someone else. We then went through a long checklist to ensure that all procedures had taken place and that I had administered all of the medication that was given to me.

I specifically mentioned that I had agreed to self-administer pain relief after the operation with my consultant. I explained what I meant and asked if this had been taken care of. I was told that they were sure it could be sorted out. I was then sitting there thinking, 'It could be sorted out? It should have been sorted; there should be no 'could' about it.'

My blood pressure was taken with the usual comment, 'It is a bit high.' I agreed with the nurse that it was down to 'white coat syndrome,' in that it increased whenever a doctor was nearby. It actually increased whenever I knew that I was going to have it taken, as I knew it was on the high side.

I got changed into a gown and sat waiting, thinking that I had packed far too much. At that time, I don't think there was anyone else in the bay of four; I was on my own. I sat quietly, and the thought of a stoma entered my mind again. What if I had to have one, and they put it in a place that was uncomfortable for me? I needed to sort this out, so I mentioned my concern to a passing nurse, who kindly arranged for a stoma nurse to come and see me.

Ten minutes later, a stoma nurse arrived and asked if she could help. I explained my thoughts to her - that if I did need one, I would like it put in a position that is good for me. I then said, 'This is not an acceptance of one or me saying that I want one, because it's not, and I don't; I just wanted to make that clear.' She laughed and said, 'Don't worry, we don't fit them for fun.' She then got a marker pen and a tape measure out.

I sat patiently waiting to be drawn on - 'X' marks the spot! After measuring the area where it would normally fit, she looked confused. She said that because I was so slight (I have a thirty inch waist and a flat stomach), she was struggling to find somewhere to put it. The only place that made any sense was my trouser line, which is where my belt fits, which is obviously no good.

Smiling to myself, I said, 'You had better warn the surgeon

that there is no room to put one then.' The nurse looked at me with a raised eyebrow and went off to explain the problem to those that count. I am sure that if push came to shove, I would have been fitted with one, but it helped that it would have been more of a problem - if 'helped' is the right word! It made me feel a bit better, anyway.

Later on, I was introduced to the 'acute pain nurse,' which sounded worrying. I discussed my chosen form of pain relief again, commenting that it had been agreed upon and that I was not going to have an epidural. I got a similar response to before, with them saying that they thought that it would be possible but would need setting up. I sat there thinking, possible? Setting up? Why hadn't it been set up? Why am I having this conversation just before my operation when it has been specifically discussed and agreed upon?

I think it must have been early to mid-morning when someone came to get me to take me down to the anaesthetist. I thought that I would be laid on a trolley and wheeled down, like I was when I had my colonoscopies. What happened was that I was escorted to a lift and taken to a lower floor. We then walked down a long, dimly lit corridor, where I found a bench to sit on and waited.

There was a guy nearby - I think he might have been a porter - who looked at me sympathetically and asked, 'Is this your first time?' I acknowledged that it was. I think I must have had the look of a rabbit in headlights about me. He said, 'Don't worry, you will be fine.' I smiled and thanked him as he left. It is surprising how a simple kind word - a word of confidence or encouragement - can make such a difference to how you feel.

I sat in a circular area with numbered doors running around it. It suddenly struck me that these were all operating theatres. It felt like I was in one of those old horror films when a door is opened and the room is splashed with blood and body parts. Probably not the best thoughts to be having at that time! My other thought was that the area desperately needed a higher-wattage lightbulb and some nice pictures to look at; it was quite dismal and gloomy.

My thoughts were thankfully interrupted by someone walking up and introducing themselves as the anaesthetist. We walked into a room, where I hopped onto a bed. I was checked again and asked various questions to ensure that they had the right person. I am pretty sure that I was given a large dose of antibiotics at this point via a cannula in my arm.

For the third time, I asked about the self-medicating pain relief that had been agreed upon after the operation. I was duly told that the usual procedure was a spinal injection. As you can imagine, I was not happy with this response, and after further discussions that bordered on arguments, I asked what the option was, as I was not prepared to have a spinal injection. We finally agreed that I would have injections around the wounds after the operation. Funnily enough, I cannot remember a thing after that! That was it; I was under. I was in the hands of the anaesthetist, the surgeon, and their team.

You know, five minutes before you are about to have a major operation, you really do not want to be lying on a trolley having an argument about pain relief! I did mention this to my consultant when I saw them next.

The next thing I remembered was hearing voices. I wasn't fully conscious, nor were my eyes open, but I could hear, 'He is starting to come around,' and later on, 'I hope they don't become infected.' I had been given the post-operation pain relief injections as agreed. Job done.

My partner had been calling to see if I was out yet and, if so, how I was. She called at half past five to be told that I was just being brought onto the ward. The operation, I am estimating, must have taken in the region of seven to eight hours. The next thing I remember is asking for a nurse because I felt sick. I was told that I had already been given some tablets to take care of that; I was given some more, thankfully. That was the last thing that I could remember until I woke up the next morning.

Day 2

As you can imagine, I was pretty sorrowful and groggy when I came around. I noticed that there was a guy in one of the beds, that I was not in pain, and that most importantly, I didn't have a stoma fitted, which was a great feeling. I breathed a huge sigh of relief. I then realised the amount of equipment attached to me - I had tubes everywhere, cannulas in my arms, and hose lines attached to my legs.

Looking around, I noticed that there were two of the type of bed that I was in and two normal beds in my bay. The one that I was lying in had monitoring equipment all around it, whereas the others were plain beds with a table next to them. I also noticed that I had a box attached to the inside of my thigh with tubes coming out of it.

It wasn't long before I was asked how I was feeling and if I was in pain, to which I replied that I felt a bit groggy, a bit sore, and was suffering with what felt like trapped wind, but I was in no pain relating to the operation itself. They carefully sat me upright rather than having me lie down, and I asked for my phone so that I could listen to something.

After a short while, the reason why I wanted to go private raised its head: the person next to me kept receiving phone calls, and rather than having his phone on vibrate, he had the ringtone on full and didn't answer it until he had listened to the ringtone in full. Thankfully, they left the ward mid-morning, and so I was on my own again - just the way I like it.

Throughout the day, I was allowed only sips of water and nothing more. Painkillers were administered, and at around three o'clock, some people came to have a chat with me in relation to getting me out of bed. I had been told that being in hospital wasn't like the old days when you lay in bed waiting to get better. Today, they wanted you out of bed and to be mobile as soon as possible because it was found to aid recovery and meant that you could vacate the bed faster, which is good for everyone.

Not long after this, a couple strolled up holding what looked like a toy and introduced themselves as physios. They explained that their role was to make sure that I was fit enough to be able to go home. To enable them to do this, they needed to see how well my lungs were performing. A stethoscope was placed on my back, and they listened to my lungs, commenting that there was some 'stickiness,' which can occur when you are laid down for long periods of time.

The 'toy' was then explained and given to me. I had to blow into a mouthpiece, which blew a ball into the air. I had to keep blowing without taking a breath to keep the ball floating between two markers for a period of time. I did okay, but they said that I should carry on doing the exercise so as to increase the capacity of my lungs. I played with it a couple of times and then dismissed it.

Late in the afternoon, the people came back to get me on my feet and asked if I was up for a short walk, to which I agreed. They spent a few minutes disconnecting things and reconnecting them when I was out of bed. I felt okay - a little wobbly and tender, but okay. I had one person on either side of me, holding onto the apparatus and me as I tentatively walked across the floor. I probably walked about fifty feet, which took me to the bay doors and back.

They asked me how I felt, and I told them that I was okay. I was then asked if I would be up for some more walking, to which I replied, 'Yes, that is not a problem, but the three of us cannot walk around together getting in everyone's way.' I said that I would be happy to walk if they disconnected me. They said that it should not be a problem if I was still up for it and was still feeling well tomorrow; they went away to discuss it.

Thankfully, to help me pass the time, I had transferred a load of music and audio books onto an old phone (the original Paddington Bear stories, Sherlock Holmes, and The Wind in the Willows), ready for when I was out of surgery and in recovery. I had no idea how secure the ward was going to be, so I took one of the old phones that we had stored away for emergencies. I wiped it clean of data, set up WhatsApp on it, and bought a pay as you go SIM card for it. It worked a treat.

I lay there listening to Rat and Moley, thinking how lucky I was that I had come through it without any immediate hitches. There wasn't, in fact, that much time that you weren't interrupted, as my blood pressure was taken every hour along with my temperature. One of the most annoying things were the pads around my calves, which took it in turns to inflate and squash one calf to then deflate while it inflated around the other calf. This process was continuous - all day and all night. There had been just one person in the bay besides me, and now that they had gone, I was the noisiest thing in there due to the air compressor and my hourly visits.

During my next blood pressure reading, I took the chance to

ask why there were different beds in the bay and what all of the apparatus was around the one that I was in, in particular the thick pads that were wrapped around my calves that seemed to be attached to some kind of compressor.

The nurse told me that I was in what is called a Cat 1 bed, which is a bed with a lot of monitoring apparatus. She told me that because I had what is known as 'dirty surgery,' it was critical that my vital signs (pulse, rate of breathing, oxygen levels, blood pressure, and body temperature) were monitored very frequently.

The reason why it is called 'dirty surgery' is that there are trillions of bacteria in the colon along with faecal matter; therefore, it was imperative that none of these got into my body via the surgery or from leakage after the operation. I remember reading in one of my letters that there was around an eight percent chance of it leaking after surgery (eight people out of every one hundred), so it is not an insignificant risk.

Due to the surgery taking place inside my body and me being sewn up and stapled together afterwards, there would be no visible sign that anything was going wrong inside of me. The only telltale sign of anything going wrong, such as leakage or infection, would be if my vital signs started to change.

Symptoms of leakage are a fever, a rapid heart rate, sepsis, a swollen, painful abdomen, delirium, shock, or if your bowels stop moving [24]. This explains why I was monitored so frequently: any change could spell trouble, and it could be big trouble - sepsis. If I caught an infection in any way, not just through leakage, I would be in an ambulance heading back to my local hospital, which takes COVID patients, and their intensive care unit. Ouch!

The next item that we discussed was the leg pads - what they were and why I had them attached to my calves. Their official title is an IPC (intermittent pneumatic compression device). Apparently, there is a risk of DVT (deep vein thrombosis), which is a blood clot usually in the lower leg or thigh, which can occur if you aren't very active for a period of time, particularly after surgery [25].

I was not aware of this, but veins, valves, and muscles in your feet and calves are often referred to as your second heart [26]; therefore, it won't be good to have them inactive for lengthy periods of time. DVT is what you can get while flying due to sitting down for so long in a cramped space.

The pads that are attached to each calf have air injected into them via a compressor every twenty or so seconds, which compresses your calf and then slowly deflates while the same happens to your other calf. Basically, the pads are compressing your calf so as to promote blood flow, much the same as walking would do. I had no idea about all of this.

They are really taking everything into account to ensure a good recovery. The problem was that this went on all of the time that you were in bed, even while you were trying to sleep. Mind you, with a nurse coming around every hour checking your vitals, there wasn't much of a chance of any sleep anyway.

The last thing to discuss was the catheter, a tube that was fed into my wiener all the way into my bladder so that I didn't have to worry about going for a pee during and after surgery. I remember hearing one of the nurses say that the readings were excellent in relation to fluid going into me via a drip as well as fluid coming out of me.

The machine strapped to my leg was monitoring how well my kidneys were performing, and by the sound of it, they were doing very well. The catheter must have been fitted after my final conversation with the anaesthetist. I am not sure who fitted it, as I wasn't conscious.

During the evening and throughout the night, an alarm kept going off around my bed; it related to my oxygen level. I know that when I sleep, my breathing can become very shallow; I even frighten myself sometimes. It is as though I have to think about breathing for it to continue.

I asked a nurse at one point what was going on, and they replied, 'It thinks that you are dead,' at which we both laughed. The alarm related to the oxygen level in my blood. A nurse kept coming to prop me up in bed, as when I slid down, my breathing became really shallow, which kept setting the alarm off.

After everything had been explained, it really hit home how

serious it all was. I was a very lucky man in so many ways: being sent the kit in the first place, the age for kits being sent out having been reduced, catching it before it had time to spread, and the care that was shown to me during all of the examinations, surgery, and aftercare.

During the night, I was pleased that I was now the only one in the bay. Early on, I started getting abdominal cramps, which worried me; it felt like really bad trapped wind. At around ten o'clock, I broke wind quite loudly due to having to push harder than usual. I am assuming this was because of the change to my bowel; it had stopped working, it had been moved about, and it was shorter now too.

I carried on breaking wind every twenty minutes or so until dawn! I was exhausted due to the constant pushing and the fact that I'd had no sleep. Can you imagine if someone else had been in there, or if I had to put up with someone breaking wind all night?

Day 3
When I saw the nurse in the morning, I mentioned what had happened during the night, and she laughed, saying that it was great news. When the bowel starts to 'fire up' again, it produces methane; therefore, if I was breaking wind all night, that meant that my gut had woken up and was preparing itself for work. I think I must have contributed to global warming that night due to the amount of greenhouse gas that I expelled from my body!

At around nine thirty, things were progressing quickly; this is only the second morning after the day of my operation. I was disconnected from all of the tubes, etc., and had long, tight elastic compression socks put on me, which replaced the IPC machine while I was mobile; I was reconnected at night when I was immobile. It was then time for my catheter to be taken out. The nurse who was assigned to me when I was first admitted had the unfortunate task of removing it.

I sat there with my gown drawn up, and she apologised for what she was going to do. I said, 'You have no need to apologise. It should be me apologising to you for what you are about to do.' She gently started pulling the tube out. After a few seconds, I said, 'Bloody hell, how much of it is there?' She laughed and said that it has to go all the way into the bladder. A few seconds later, it was all done. There was no tube inside me, and there was no box strapped to my leg.

Funnily enough, I wasn't starving hungry, even though I had not eaten for days, but I was glad to be told that I could have something small to eat. That turned out to be the best tasting white buttered toast that I have ever had; it was so nice to be able to eat something.

I sat next to my bed with my little food trolley and did as I was instructed, eating slowly and chewing plenty before swallowing. To wash it down, I had a cup of tea, which was equally as good. I was starting to feel normal again. To my surprise, I was then offered a very small amount of rice cereal and milk, which was followed by a second cup of tea. It felt like I was at a restaurant. It was superb.

I have said before that when you are ill or down on your luck, the smallest things can bring such a smile to your face, and boy did they. I felt like a king.

A lot of trust is put in what you say, as I was asked by the tea person what I would like to eat and given options that were fibrous (contained fibre). I knew that I should not be eating anything with too much fibre in it, as it could overload my bowels. It needed simple food - food that it could break down and move along easily. I thought there would be an old-fashioned clipboard at the end of each bed telling those who needed to know what patients could and could not have.

When I had finished eating, I was feeling so upbeat that I delved into my bag and got my shampoo, body wash, wipes, and towel out, along with some clothes. After speaking to the nurse and agreeing to take it easy, I trotted off to the washroom and gave myself a very slow and careful flannel wash. As I disrobed, I saw the dressings (large, clear, waterproof plasters) that covered my wounds for the first time. When I told the nurse what I was doing, she said not to worry about the dressings as they were showerproof, but I kept water away from them anyway.

While washing around my bottom, to my surprise, I felt movement in my bowel. After wiping the toilet seat down with antibacterial wipes, I sat on it and actually went to the toilet. What little came out was a strange green colour, but it was solid. This was what had been left over from before the surgery; there was no way that the food that I had just eaten had been digested that quickly. It was a very encouraging sign though, although my pee was also a strange sage green colour. I am not sure what was going on with everything being a weird shade of green.

I was still feeling okay on my feet and felt invigorated after my hearty breakfast. I had told myself that there was no rush, so I washed my hair too. I then abandoned my gown, gave myself a spray of deodorant, and put on a t-shirt along with underwear, socks, shorts, and finally a baseball cap. Like the breakfast, it was just another step closer to normality and life as it used to be. This was made all the better when I walked out into the corridor and all of the nurses at the nurse's station shouted, 'Yey, he's back.' It was a great feeling. I took a bow, albeit gently.

After all the excitement, I sat on my bed, put my headphones on, and listened to some Sherlock Holmes. After about an hour, I thought that I would go for a walk. I started with a circuit around the bay that I was in, taking it nice and steady. While nosing around, I found a snug room, so I sat in there out of the way for a while, enjoying some peace and quiet. While I sat there, it suddenly dawned on me that I had felt little to no pain since the operation. I know that I had injections after I came out of surgery, but I was feeling nothing apart from a little tenderness.

So far, I hadn't used the phone to make calls as having cannulas in my arms made it difficult; therefore, I used WhatsApp a lot, messaging backwards and forwards to my partner. I was limited in who I sent messages to, as I had not told anyone what had happened to me or where I was except for the friend who followed us to the hospital. At this point, I looked through the contacts on my phone and chose a few people to message to let them know what was going on.

Now I was clear of the operation, and even though it was very early days, I felt better in relation to my position, which made me more relaxed discussing it. I felt better talking about it, even if it was just by text or WhatsApp.

The response that I had to my messages was one of shock, as no one expected it - as I hadn't! While in the room, my phone pinged, and it was my friend who was telling me about their night out. COVID rules had been relaxed, and so they had been out for a drink and to listen to some music. On the way home, while riding their bike, they told me that they must have been a bit worse for wear because they had crashed their bike and fallen over someone's wall in front of an audience. I sat in the room, howling with laughter. What a star. A laugh was just what I needed.

I spoke to the nurses about the possibility of tucking into some of my biscuits or some boiled sweets, and they said that it was okay to eat them as long as I didn't go overboard. The thought of some chocolate brought a smile to my face. I had put some sweets in my pocket beforehand, so I sucked on a couple while I sat reading the news on my phone.

After depressing myself reading the news, I thought I would

walk another circuit. Just around the corner, I found a door leading to some stairs. The door was not locked, so I opened it, and there were four or five flights of stairs, each with around ten steps. Why not? I thought. I gently placed my foot on the first step and ascended step by step. I did this for the first flight and then walked down, step by step. It all went rather well - not even a twinge. I did it again, and I felt fine. I thought that I had better give it up after two flights, and so I walked around the corner back to the snug room. I really was spoiled to have this little haven all to myself.

After a while, I heard the tea trolley and so walked back to my bay, where dinner was being served. I had a thin slice of white fish and some mash, followed by another cup of tea. It was fantastic. Not long after this, I felt the need to pee, which was the first time since my catheter had been removed. At the same time, I felt movement in my bowels again and so pottered off to the toilet; I passed the same as before. Nonetheless, it was an encouraging sign, for which I was grateful.

Each time I went, I told one of the nurses. I felt like a school kid reporting to their teacher, 'Miss, I have been to the loo again!' The only thing that I found odd was that no one came to take a look at what had come out. I thought they might want to see what it was like.

The other positive thing was that there was no sign of blood. Even after I had been sent home, I never saw any blood after going to the loo. You are told to keep an eye out for signs of blood, as there could be some discharge due to the surgery, but it should not be continuous, and there should not be more than a certain amount. Later on, during my recovery, I had a bit of a heart attack at one point as I had a quick glance at my stools and noticed red blotches. I quickly took a closer look to see that the red patches were, in fact, bits of tomato skin!

I must admit that I was worried about going for a pee, as I thought that it might be like it was after my cystoscopy – absolute bloody agony! Thankfully, it wasn't; it was just a little sore. I had a bit of blood around the tip of my wiener, which was probably due to having the catheter fitted. I told the nurse, and she told me to drink plenty of water; it would help flush my system out and make the passing of water easier. I took her advice, and it did exactly that: listen to your nurse!

While I was around the nurse's station, the main consultant came around and had a quick chat with me, telling me how pleased he was with my progress. We briefly discussed how long people stay in hospital after such an operation. I was told that each person is different and that, ideally, they like to see someone having gone to the loo properly before they leave to make sure that the bowel is functioning correctly.

If the bowel became blocked or stopped functioning, then it could be a matter of waiting, not eating or drinking, with the possibility of being sick. I must admit, I discussed being sick with the colorectal nurses before I was admitted, as I have very strong stomach muscles that go into an uncontrollable spasm when I am sick. This would not bode well after having just had my abdomen stitched and stapled back up!

I was reminded that if I was discharged and anything went wrong, then I would have to go to my local A&E, as I would not be allowed back where I was due to not being swabbed and their non-COVID policy. The thought of going to another hospital worried me greatly, as I had settled into this one and had pretty much had the bay to myself.

During the afternoon, I kept myself busy by walking circuits of the ward and extending my range up the stairs. I wasn't sure whether I was allowed there or not. A nurse passed me and said nothing, so I assumed that it was okay. This time, I walked up all the flights of stairs to the top.

It was odd; it was like a disused part of the building where files were stored. I was waiting to get kicked out at any point! I walked back down to where I had started to find that the door had been closed and I needed a code to get back in - I had been locked out! This was embarrassing. After loitering about for ten minutes, the door opened. I smiled with relief and walked back onto my ward and back into the snug room again.

It wasn't long before I heard the tea trolley rattling its way down the corridor, so I pulled my earphones out and went to see what was on the menu that evening. I chose mushroom soup and some white, buttered toast. The soup tasted like it had been made from powder and was pretty gross. I had a few sips from my cup of tea, and all I could taste was fluoridated water, so I gave it up as a bad job. I had done well up until then, so I wasn't complaining.

The conversation with the consultant was worrying me (if my bowel stops or is blocked), and so I asked one of the nurses if I could have a chat. We sat near my bed, and I explained how I thought and how that led to me asking questions. I was not in control; therefore, I needed to understand what was going on so that I could make sense of it.

I had never been in a position where my life was in someone else's hands and I had virtually no input. I explained that I was worried about my bowels not working. She was lovely and very understanding. She could see that I was getting upset and reassured me that becoming emotional can be an after-effect of the anaesthetic.

I told her I was concerned that I couldn't hear anything happening below; normally, you can hear your bowels gurgling and grumbling as food and liquid travel through them. She quickly took her stethoscope out, put the ear pieces in my ears, and placed the pad on my abdomen. I said that all I could hear was a static noise, to which she replied, 'That is the sound of your bowels working.'

My next question was, 'Why are foods that we are normally told not to eat on the list of foods to eat?' The reply was that simple foods such as white pasta and white bread are easy for the bowel to grab hold of and move. What you don't want to happen is for the bowel to be overtaxed early on, which could then lead to it shutting down or a blockage being created. If high-fibre foods were eaten, they could overtax the bowel as they require far more work to break down.

The final question that I asked (she was very patient, bless her, and I do) was, 'Why did I take so many antibiotics and other drugs the same day that I took laxatives? Won't they just be flushed out?' The reason I was given so much was just for that reason. Knowing that a proportion will be flushed away with the laxative, you are given a lot more than normal so that a certain amount will still stay in your body. I was very grateful for the nurse taking the time to explain things to me. I felt much better and more confident after our discussion.

After a few more circuits around the ward and reading notices on the walls, I retired back to the snug room, where I carried on messaging people and reading the news on my phone. I wanted to stay there as long as possible in the hope that I might be tired enough to get a decent night's sleep.

I had retired back to my bed late in the evening when a nurse came around with the usual painkillers and to take my readings and blood pressure. I was duly told off for lying with my legs crossed again, as it can restrict blood flow. I asked if the painkillers were to stop inflammation (anti-inflammatory), and she said that they were not; they were just for pain. I said that I had no pain, so I didn't see the point in taking them; from then on, I didn't take any.

My blood pressure was taken again, and the usual comment was made that it was on the high side, but this time, I was told that a letter would be sent to my GP asking them to arrange an appointment to discuss it with me. I think my excuses have worn thin!

Earlier on, I overheard discussions about trying to place a patient at another hospital as they either didn't have the room or they needed treatment and care that couldn't be provided. I will explain that I wasn't being nosey, as the nurse's station was in the middle of the bays and the bay doors were always open; therefore, you could pretty much hear everything that went on. The lights were always on too, which, all told, means that getting any sleep is almost impossible.

Shift change took place, and there was much discussion relating to this poor person who was still waiting to be relocated. One of the doctors said that they would stay with the nurse in charge until a hospital could be found to take the patient. In the early hours of the morning, all I could hear was the patient being sick and the nurses comforting them. Those in charge were desperately trying to find this poor person a place. This went on for hours, but after many phone calls and conversations, a place was eventually found.

It was a real eye-opener as to how pressured the NHS is and how the nursing staff work so tirelessly to look after us all. The bizarre thing was that at two thirty in the morning, a nurse asked me if I wanted a hot drink and took my blood pressure. At around four o'clock in the morning, peace reigned again, and all was calm. So much for a quiet night!

Day 4

My fourth day started with me packing my bags, as I had heard on the grapevine that it was likely that I would be discharged that day. Not long after my breakfast, I received a visit from the consultant in charge. He started our conversation with, 'What is that down there?' pointing at my packed bags, followed by, 'Where do you think you are going? Are you not happy with our five-star accommodation?'

I explained that I had heard that I would be discharged today. He smiled and said in all seriousness that this was the third day after the day that I had major surgery, the emphasis being on major surgery. If I was allowed to go home and something happened, then I would be on my own. I could not come back, and I would find myself in A&E at my local hospital.

The normal recovery time for such an operation was four to five days, and even then, most people had not recovered to the extent that I had. The worry was that because I was doing so well, I could cause a rupture. If this happened and it caused a leak, then I could be in real trouble. Even though I had made a remarkable recovery, for the sake of one more day, he would prefer that I stay under observation.

He also said that if he let me go, with me having spent such a short recovery time in hospital, and something went wrong, it would reflect badly on him and his judgement. I fully understood and said that I would adhere to whatever he said; another day was not going to make a difference to me.

This was my first major stay in hospital, and I found it interesting how quickly I became accustomed to being looked after. I am not saying that I took advantage, because I did not. What I am trying to say is that it was like having a comfort blanket wrapped around me; it gave me a feeling of security and safety.

What I didn't want to happen was to lose that feeling, especially as I had gotten to know the nurses and the people that looked after me. As daft as it may sound, I can honestly imagine people wanting to stay in hospital just for this reason, and I would not be surprised if that happened.

While I had his attention, I asked if my second CT scan, which had been taken around three weeks prior to my operation, was clear. By clear, I meant that there was no other sign of cancer anywhere - that there were no signs of it having spread to other organs. His answer was that it was clear, to which I gave a sigh of relief and thanked him again for everything that had been done for me.

The first thing I did was message my partner to let her know what was going on. Obviously, we were both disappointed, but there was no point in putting myself at risk for the sake of one more day.

Now that I knew I was going to be around for another day, I

tucked into another helping of fish and mash. I had grown to quite like it. To pass the time, I went off to the toilet to have a wash and brush up; it always makes me feel better.

On the way back, I asked a nurse what happened to the dressings covering my incisions. She replied that either a district nurse could come and change them for me or that I could go to my GP, and a nurse would have a look at my wounds and change my dressings. Not wanting to waste a district nurse's time, I said that I would pop to my GP; it wasn't a problem.

While she was with me, she asked what the yellow thing was on my bed. I explained that the physiotherapist had dropped it off for me to practice with. She then told me that the physiotherapist would have a say in whether I was allowed home or not, so I had better make sure that I could do as he had asked. I didn't know this, so I started puffing on the toy to make the ball hover!

After a stint of blowing into the toy, I put a couple of biscuits in my pocket and disappeared in search of the stairs again. I climbed them several times from top to bottom and then walked around the ward, looking at posters that I had already read. I eventually got bored and went back to my bed, listening to Paddington while making notes for my book. I was writing a book about humanity and the climate crisis. This kept me busy until teatime, when I had scrambled egg sandwiches and some of my squash.

In the evening, a male nurse came around to check my vitals, and I was explaining what had been agreed upon today in relation to me leaving. I was a little surprised when he told me that they wanted me kept in until I had been to the toilet properly, i.e., I had passed a fresh stool and not one that was from before I had my operation. This obviously came as a shock to me, and I wondered if this was the case - why hadn't someone told me? It is a logical thing to ask for - to make sure that my bowels were functioning correctly before I left. I would not have argued.

The evening passed by without incident, apart from a nurse deciding to do a stocktake around midnight. I lay there listening to boxes and bottles being shuffled about while wondering whether I would actually be going home tomorrow.

When the stocktake had finished, I took it upon myself to see if I could help my bowels by not just lying flat on my back. I hadn't heard a gurgling sound for some time and wondered whether I could help it along by altering the pressure on my bowels. After lying on my back, I gently turned my body on its side for fifteen minutes. When you change the position of your body, internal organs move, and my hope was that as I moved from my back to my side, pressure on my bowels would change, helping the movement of anything inside them.

Within those fifteen minutes, I heard a gurgle and a rumble. This was the first time since I'd had the operation that I had heard my bowels, apart from breaking wind all night and through the nurse's stethoscope! I then turned to lying flat on my back again, which should change the pressure again. After a few minutes, I heard another rumble and felt something move. I then shuffled onto my other side for fifteen minutes and had the same reaction. I carried on rotating my body for a couple of hours, and the sounds were very encouraging. I was sufficiently tired by then to get a much-needed few hours of sleep.

The fifth, and what turned out to be my final day, turned out to be a day of confusion, followed by me passing some blood while peeing. I told the nurse what had happened and that it was also painful when peeing. The nurse requested a pee sample so that it could be tested to see if I had an infection, as the catheter could have caused some damage. I had only just been, so that was not going to be easy. I ended up drinking a huge jug of horrible tasting tap water to try and get things moving.

Within the hour, I was trotting off to the loo again to see if there was any sign of blood or if it still hurt. The good news was that there was no sign of blood, and the more I peed, the more the pain dissipated. Again, listen to the nurse; they know best. She told me the best thing I could do was drink lots of water to help flush my waterways out.

After eating my breakfast of toast and marmalade, followed by rice cereal and a cup of tea, I laid on my bed with my baseball cap over my face. Shortly after, the test results of my pee came back: there was no infection, which was great news.

Believe it or not, I actually refused a body wash in the shower by a nurse, mainly because there was a lot going on and I wanted to be around. It was a shame. I would have enjoyed that, I'm sure.

Mid-morning, a doctor came up to me and asked how I was, and so I told them about my pee sample, that I was waiting to go to the loo to provide a fresh stool sample, and that I thought this to be sensible. After all, the last thing I wanted was to have a blocked bowel or a problem with my bowel not functioning correctly and end up at my local A&E. They agreed with what I had said and confirmed that I really should show my bowels to be working before being released.

Confusion was rife as, later in the morning, a consultant introduced himself to me as a part of the team that operated on me, for which I thanked him. He asked me a few questions, and I said that I was waiting to pass a fresh stool before being released. I was told that I did not need to do that here and that I would be going home today! I was a little shocked by this, especially having my comfort blanket pulled from beneath me. I had settled on the fact that I needed to prove everything was working before I was released, rather than being released with my fingers crossed that nothing would go wrong!

To make my day, as if on cue, shortly after my conversation with the consultant, I felt movement in my bowels, and so off

I went to the loo. This was another good result in that I had gone to the loo properly; I had produced a fresh stool from the food that I had eaten since the operation. I went off to the nurse's station, telling them what I thought was headline grabbing news.

The funny thing was that no one checked; no one said to me that they needed to be told when I had been to the loo properly so that they could come and check. In essence, I could have gone into the toilet, waited five minutes, came out, and told them that I had produced a fresh stool; no one would have been any the wiser.

So, I had done everything requested of me; what next? Well, the physiotherapist came around and asked how I was. I told him that I had been walking circuits around the ward, that I had conducted a couple of body washes by myself as well as washing my hair, and that I had been climbing the stairs. He said that I had made great progress but never asked to see me walking or climbing the stairs, which I thought was odd; it was another example of just taking my word for it.

I asked the physio about my compression socks and whether I could take them off. He confirmed that due to my high level of mobility, there was no reason for me to keep them on, as they were really for people with little or no mobility. I honestly cannot remember whether my lungs were checked again or whether they asked me to blow into the yellow toy again. The end result of the meeting was that I was passed as being fit enough to be discharged.

For some reason, I skipped dinner. I think I was so excited and upskittled at the same time that I couldn't afford the time or energy to spend eating. It was a shame, as it was my favourite - fish and mash! I was happy that I had proven my bowels were functioning properly and that I had passed no blood either. My mind was now fixed on going home!

A nurse came around later on and asked why I didn't have my compression socks on. I told them that the physiotherapist had told me that I didn't need to wear them and explained why, to which I was told in no uncertain terms that I was to put them back on and that I had to wear them for three weeks. It really didn't matter to me either way; I just wanted to know whether to wear them or not. I did as I was told and put them back on!

It seemed busier that day; there were more people being admitted, and the nurses were under pressure having to deal with people leaving as well as people arriving. This was not made any easier when a guy came into my bay (I call it my bay, as I was the only person in it for the duration of my stay other than the morning after my operation) wreaking of cigarettes.

I was lying on my bed with my baseball cap over my face, listening to what was going on around me. I looked up and saw the nurse holding the new guy's medical file, which looked more like a door stopper - it was about four inches thick! No wonder my consultant asked me if there was something missing from mine as it only had one page in it.

The next minute, he had disappeared, and the nurse was asking where he had gone. I told her that I didn't know, but I could guess - to have a cigarette! At that point, cursing, she stormed off to try to find him. Ten minutes later, he returned, smelling of cigarette smoke!

If I were a nurse, or anyone else in the NHS for that matter, I would be angry too. The amount of money and time that is spent treating people who really don't care about their health must be astronomical. It is not just the money, but the pressure put on the health system too; I think it is grossly unfair for people to act in this way. If they want to ignore what they have been told, then leave them to it. Why should we all have to pay and suffer for their selfishness?

A different nurse caught my attention this time, one saying that she needed to get my medication sorted out before my papers were signed. I explained that I had found them in a drawer next to my bed; no one had told me, I just found them while I was exploring. They expressed relief that it had been done and started to walk off. I called, 'Aren't you going to check them?' They turned around and did so; after all, someone could have helped themselves to some, or they might not all have been there.

I had a bagful again: boxes upon boxes of flavoured drinks, anticoagulant syringes, painkillers (paracetamol and ibuprofen), and gastroprotection tablets should I take the ibuprofen that I was given. The drinks were high calorie and high protein drinks; 200ml contained 400kcal. To put this into perspective, a bottle of fizzy drink that I had contained just 48kcal per 200ml. The high calorie drinks also contained vitamins and minerals.

For some reason, I thought they were specific to healthcare providers, but they can be bought easily enough on the Internet and from retailers. I stopped taking painkillers when I was in hospital, so I saw little point in taking them at home. I kept them for personal use, with a reminder on the ibuprofen packets to only take one tablet instead of two, as they were twice the strength of the normal ones that we bought.

When I was told that I was definitely going home and that all I needed were my discharge papers to be signed, I messaged my partner, asking her if she could bring a pillow for the journey home. The pillow was not for me to sit on, but for me to put in front of my stomach to protect it from the seatbelt, especially if we had to brake hard.

Two o'clock came, and I went to the nurse's station and thanked them all for their care, for putting up with me, and for looking after me. I was quite emotional as my comfort blanket was being taken away, but on the other hand, I had proven that my bowels were working as they should, and I was desperate to see my partner. Due to COVID restrictions, she had not been allowed to visit me.

I could see the short-stay parking lot out of a window and said that I would be waving from a window on the first floor

- little did I know that the glass was mirrored on the outside!

After what seemed like forever, I saw her park up, and a nurse came down with me to help carry my medication and bag.

Once we had both thanked her, we threw ourselves into each other's arms and stood embracing in floods of tears for what seemed like a lifetime. We eventually parted and loaded the car, and I sat in the front with my pillow over my lap. Home James, and don't spare the horses!

5

Recovery at home

My partner took a week off work to see me settled and to make sure that I was going to be okay on my own. As a part of my recovery at home, I had to inject myself with an anticoagulant each day for around three weeks to help prevent blood clotting. These were the same injections that I had whilst I was in the hospital.

It was the same procedure that I had to carry out the day before my operation. I had to pinch some flesh about two inches to the side of my belly button and then slowly press the needle in as far as it would go while still maintaining the pinch of flesh. When it had been pushed all the way in, if you pushed hard enough, you would hear a click. The click is a cover that shoots out, enclosing the needle.

I set an alarm on my phone to go off at eight o'clock every evening to remind me. When the alarm went off, I hauled myself upstairs to give myself an injection. I had to alternate sides each day and try not to inject myself in the same place. Once I had finished, I placed the syringe in a special yellow container that I had been given along with my medication. When I had completed my injections, I had to write my details on the label of the box and take the box to my GP so that the syringes could be disposed of safely. I felt a bit like a pin cushion at the end of it. I cannot say that it ever hurt; it just became a bind.

Besides injecting myself, I had to take my temperature three times a day, as changes in body temperature can indicate infection. I soon found a good digital thermometer on the Internet that you place under your tongue, and then I found out what temperature range was classified as normal: around 37°C seemed to be the norm, but it can range from 36.1°C to 37.2°C [27]. I was within the range, so I was okay. If I was unsure, I would take another reading.

I always thought that a high temperature was an indicator of an infection, but having a low temperature can also be an indicator [28].

As well as the above, I had to keep my compression socks on, which I duly did, even at night. They lasted about two weeks before they completely disintegrated. To be honest, I'd had enough of them by then. There was nothing else to do apart from let my body recover and not overdo things.

When I was home, I could relax and take it easy - no oxygen or pulse alarms going off or pressure pads attached to my legs; it was heaven. I started a walking regime to increase my fitness and to enjoy the fresh air. Every day I would look to go a little further, but I was careful not to overdo it. I was warned at the hospital that everything was still healing and that if I overdid things, I could end up with a hernia, which would mean another visit to the hospital and possible complications.

The first day that I was home, we walked to the end of the

road and back again in the evening, with me wearing a pair of baggy pyjama bottoms that had an elastic waist. My wounds were still tender, and I did not want to put pressure on them by wearing a heavy pair of jeans and a belt. I went out in the evening, as it was quiet and it was unlikely that I would be seen shuffling up and down the street. I still hadn't told anyone what I had been through, not even our neighbours.

The next day, I turned left at the top of the road and went halfway down the long road and back home. Bear in mind that I was walking around the house and up and down flights of stairs during the day to get to the toilet too. By the weekend, I had completed a full circuit around the block, which is around half a mile.

With regards to food, I was given a list when I left the hospital of what I could eat and what I shouldn't eat. A couple of phrases that were repeated to me by nurses were 'little and often' and 'don't overdo it.' Bear in mind that it has been less than a week since I had the operation, so my bowel is still pretty annoyed at what has happened to it. I stuck to a routine of cheesy mash and chicken for dinner and cheesy mash and a small piece of white fish for tea.

If I was hungry between meals, I would have some buttered white toast with jam or marmalade on it or a biscuit. I set my trusty alarm again for nine o'clock, one o'clock, and six o'clock, so that my bowel became used to eating the same food at the same time. I wanted to get it into a routine. I didn't want to give it any shocks or surprises!

The routine seemed to work well, as when I went to the toilet, my stools were the best that they had ever been, and I was going regularly - around the same time every day. Things were looking good. One thing that I learned was to go when I felt movement in my bowel and to let it happen by itself, not to push. I could hold it if I really needed to, but what happened was that when I did go, I then had to push, I got stomach cramps, and it wasn't as straightforward as it would have been if I had gone when my body told me to.

I was on this diet for around three months before I could start to expand it. I was just happy to be alive, not to have a stoma, and to still be able to go to the loo properly. I had leaflets given to me saying that my stools may be runny and that I could pass blood clots due to my bowel clearing blood from the operation. I am pleased to say that I did not experience either of those after-effects.

Within two weeks of leaving the hospital, I went to see the nurse at my local medical centre to have my dressings checked. Out of the four, only one showed a little patch of blood on it. As the nurse peeled the dressings back, I saw the incisions for the first time. The dressings were duly changed with spare ones that the hospital had given me, and I was good to go. While I was there, I asked about driving and was told that it was really down to me and whether I felt safe and comfortable to drive; they didn't have a say in it.

I remember speaking to one of the colorectal nurses before I had my operation, who told me that a rule of thumb was about six weeks to drive and twelve weeks to get back to normal activities, but to keep in mind that everyone is different.

With this in mind, when I got home, I spoke to my insurer for guidance. Unfortunately, I got through to someone who clearly did not know what they were talking about, as I was told that I had to get a certificate from my doctor. What is my doctor going to do - sit with me in the car and check how my driving is?

I made a quick phone call to a colorectal nurse, and I understood why they said six weeks before driving. I mistakenly thought that it was to do with the seatbelt putting pressure on my wounds should I have an accident or have to stop quickly. What it actually had to do with was how fast I could react to a situation where I needed to stop quickly. How fast could I raise my foot to then stamp on the brake pedal and maintain that pressure?

If you think about it, you will use your stomach muscles when braking hard, and the last thing that you want to happen is to be in pain while stamping on the brake pedal, as your body's immediate reaction will be to reduce the pain by reducing the pressure that you are applying.

Now that I understood what it was about, I called my insurer again and got through to someone who did know what they were talking about. I was assured that what had been said previously was incorrect and that, provided I felt safe, there was no reason why I could not drive. With this in mind and a huge smile on my face, I went to get my car's key fob.

It was nice to sit behind the steering wheel again. We do like our cars, don't we? I nimbly reversed out of our driveway and slowly drove down the road. I tried a couple of sharp stops, and I was fine. The seatbelt did not hurt, and I was not in any pain when I jumped on the brake. I was good to go.

I didn't tend to venture very far to start with, and only to places that I knew had good toilet facilities. This had nothing to do with driving, but with my confidence. Even though my bowel habits had settled down and I was pretty regular, the last thing that I wanted to happen was to get 'caught short,' especially whilst out with my partner. It just needed a bit of thought as to where and when we went somewhere.

Ideally, I would make sure that I went to the loo before we went out. I did this by sticking to a routine every morning. I would have a couple of chocolate biscuits, a mug of tea, and a bowl of cereal, which would get things moving. I wouldn't hang around eating it, either.

If I needed to help things along, I knew that a little extra pressure applied around my stomach area, which I could create by tightening my belt by one hole would do the trick.

I am not recommending that you do this. I only did it when

everything was well and truly healed, and it was something that I was used to doing. It is difficult because if I did not go on time and missed a day, I would start to worry that things had stopped working or that there was a blockage, and so I felt pressure to go each day and to keep my bowel movements as regular as I could for my mental state, probably more than my physical state.

I did have one incident where I had a blockage; I literally could not push it out, and the last thing that you want to be doing during recovery is pushing too hard. I am afraid, to put it bluntly, I had to 'get down and dirty' and manually help it out! When you are faced with something like this, I am afraid you just have to bite your lip and get on with it. That was the only time that I had such an issue, and thankfully, I was at home when it happened.

There is a nature reserve a few miles away, which I drove to and walked around to help build up my walking distance and stamina. I started on a short trail of around two miles, working my way up to just over three miles. The walking and fresh air did me the world of good, both physically and mentally. It was good to be alive and to be a part of things again.

Another couple of weeks passed by, and I went back to see the nurse and had the staples and stitches removed and the incisions inspected. Everything was fine, so I left dressing free and was now happy to have a shower rather than a hand wash. Another step closer to normality!

Six weeks after my operation, I thought that I would try one of my 'normal activities,' which was horse riding (dressage). My partner and I discussed it, and I said that it would just be nice to get back in the saddle again, even if I spent the lesson just walking about. On arrival, I got my horse and used a mounting block to get on. I then got comfortable by adjusting my stirrups. We walked around for a few minutes, and then we broke into a steady trot. All was well.

I carried on the lesson as I would normally; just having a walk went out of the window, I'm afraid. I did feel okay though; no twinges, no pain, just the delight of getting back to normal. The one thing that I had to be careful of was dismounting, as I was dropping from a height and needed to have a clean dismount. I rode weekly until the start of my chemotherapy. It helped both my confidence and my level of fitness.

During my conversations with consultants and colorectal nurses, the possibility of having to have chemotherapy did raise its head; it was not uncommon with this type of cancer. Shortly after having my dressings changed, I received a letter asking me to attend a video meeting with a consultant in relation to exactly that.

The day of the video conference came, and my partner and I sat in front of my laptop, having logged into the NHS portal, waiting for the consultant to join us. We sat there for nearly fifty minutes, and then my phone rang. It was the consultant's secretary saying that the video meeting had been cancelled.

This was the start of my not-so-happy relationship with this particular consultant!

Before my chemotherapy meeting, I received a letter, which probably explained why I was put forward for the treatment. Earlier on, I gave my readings as T2 N0 MO. These had now changed to (TNM 8): pT2 pN1a M0.

From what I can gather, the main difference between the initial readings and the new readings, which were taken from the analysis of the tumour and tissues taken out of my body, is that a cancer cell or cells were found in a nearby lymph node; in all, eighteen lymph nodes were taken out. The cell(s), however, were said not to be assessable, meaning that no information could be gleaned from them.

So, as far as I am aware, the cancer has not spread to the outer wall of the colon, no signs have been found of a cancer anywhere else (it has not spread), and a cancer cell(s) has been found in a lymph node. I think it kind of leaves me in the middle in relation to the risk of further development - not at the bottom, but not at the top.

The fact that it had not spread to the outer wall of the colon is important, as they found that my colon had shown signs of adhesion to the inside of my abdominal wall. If it had spread to the outer wall, then it could have easily spread to my abdominal wall.

The last thing that happened before I started chemotherapy

was a meeting with a consultant. My partner and I turned up around fifteen minutes early. The clock ticked past our appointment time, and around fifteen minutes later, we were called in. I had my weight checked, and then we were left by ourselves to find the consultant's office. We sat down, and they talked about the treatment and why it had been put forward. The treatment was described as not being 'a walk in the park,' which I did not expect it to be.

The meeting turned to my previous appointments, who they were with, and when they took place. I could not give dates and names as I had not been asked to provide that kind of information, and to be honest, I thought that it would be on their computer anyway. I was then told that I should remember the names of the people who do important things for me in my life! I think at this point my blood pressure was close to my mum's at over 200! I was absolutely furious!

My partner at this point was in tears, and I really felt like letting off some steam, but as this person was in charge of my treatment, I didn't want to rock the boat or be transferred to someone else and lose time. To make matters worse, they said that I must be pretty fed up that I had it (cancer), being physically fit and a non-smoker, as well as being tea total! At this point, my fists were clenched, and I was a lighter shade of purple.

As I always had time on my mind in relation to treatment, I asked if I could begin my treatment sooner. I was told that it usually starts around ten weeks after the operation so that the body has time to recover. This was not just to do with the operation but more to prepare itself for chemotherapy, as it too will take its toll. The body needs to be fit, healthy, and resilient if it is going to withstand twelve weeks of chemotherapy.

The treatment that I was going to have had many possible side-effects, one of which was death. I was given pamphlets listing them all. I briefly scanned through the four pages and was horrified at some of the side-effects. I was given time to read through and understand the possible outcomes and ramifications of having the treatment before I started it. I quickly glanced through the pages and signed the patient agreement form, confirming that I agreed to have the treatment. We left it at that, and I said that I would wait to hear from them. We went home very angry at how we had been treated and talked to.

When we arrived home, I sat and read through the side-effects and was mortified - they could be temporary; they could be permanent; they could be life changing; they could be life ending! It is a little bit like when I spoke with the first anaesthetists, who told me the odds of dying while under anaesthesia. In that instance, I told them that I really didn't have a choice because if I didn't have the operation, I would die. In this instance, I did have a choice, but in my mind, I really didn't.

Due to one of my lymph nodes having been found to have a cancer cell or cells in it, there was a risk that other cancer cells might have travelled elsewhere in my lymph system. I had been told that a CT scan was not able to detect singular cancer cells; therefore, if I did not have chemotherapy and cells had escaped, then I could end up with cancer elsewhere - metastasis. This was not a risk that I was prepared to take. In my mind, I just had to 'suck it up' and get on with it.

It is a balance of risk, isn't it? You either take the risk of the countless side-effects and what they could do to you, or you decide not to have the treatment and risk cancer starting elsewhere if cancer cells have escaped.

About a week later, I had another ECG to make sure that all was well with my heart before I started therapy. I also had another blood pressure test and got the usual response. However, this time I was able to say that I had been referred to my GP and that it was being taken care of. I had actually spoken to my GP about it, as the hospital had written to him, and we agreed that it would be best to leave it until after I'd had chemotherapy. There was no point in adding something else into the equation at this stage.

One of the nurses told me not to listen to other people's experiences of chemotherapy, as literally everyone has a different experience. If this is the case, you are probably wondering why I am telling you about my experience. I think it is relevant, and even though people may experience different side-effects or have a different journey, it is interesting to understand the process and to hear what other people have been through. After all, the information relating to side-effects came from people like me and countless others. I think it helps prepare you for what lies ahead; it gives you an idea of the possibilities.

The date for when my chemotherapy was going to start came through, and it is sod's law that it coincided with the re-booking of our holiday again. I emailed the hotel and explained my position and that I would fully understand if they could not accommodate another change. To my delight, they told me that they would wait for me to confirm another date. How lovely was that? We made sure that when we finally did go away, we saw the person involved, took them a large bouquet of flowers, and told them how grateful we were for their understanding and patience.

One other thing that I told my partner needed to be done was to get our nearest and dearest around to tell them, as I could not get away with being absent for another three months! With this in mind, I messaged various friends, saying, 'We have something to tell you.' This did the trick, and dates were put in the diary for them to come and see us.

While I was at it, I also contacted the care home where mum was and had a chat with them to explain that I would not be around for three months and why. I could have risked going, but the care home had already had a number of COVID outbreaks, and mum had already had it; thankfully, she was okay. I knew that chemotherapy can have a detrimental effect on your immune system and make you more susceptible to illness should you catch a bug. There was no way that I was going to put my treatment or my health at risk; I am afraid that mum would have to wait!

I would say that this was one of the hardest things that I had to do - confront friends and loved ones to explain what had happened as well as what was about to happen. I told them what I had been diagnosed with, details about my operation, and what lay ahead: chemotherapy.

The reason why I had kept it quiet also had to be explained: that I needed to know where I stood and what the future was before I told anyone. Once I was over the first hurdle of explaining what I had been diagnosed with, it became a little easier, but every now and then my partner had to step in and take over as I was becoming too upset to talk. I found it very traumatic and extremely upsetting.

I felt like a harbinger of bad news, especially as one of the couples who came to see us had already each lost a parent to cancer, and now I had been tarred with it.

Although much of what is written is about what I went through, how it affected me, and how I felt, there must be no illusion that my partner had an easy ride because she didn't have the disease and I did. It could not be further from the truth. Her life had been turned upside down, as had mine, and for my sake, she bit her lip and hid her emotions from me the best that she could, as she knew that if I saw her upset, then I would become upset too. Don't get me wrong; there were many times when we were in each other's arms in floods of tears as one or the other found it too much to cope with.

The mental side of both having and coping with this disease and its treatments is not to be underestimated. This relates to the people who have it as well as the people that surround them, such as family, partners, and friends; everyone is affected.

This is one reason why I have taken the time to write this book - it is as much for the people who are close to the patient as it is for the patient themselves. Be under no illusion; those who have to deal with knowing that a loved one has been diagnosed with it will be going through the ringer themselves. It is hard on everyone - very hard.

I could never have gotten through it without her. The fact is that I most likely owe her my life due to her having the strength and love to make me take the test in the first place! As I said early on, I was going to throw it in the bin and had left it sitting on the worktop for three weeks. I still kick myself for doing this, as if I hadn't, it might not have developed from stage 2 to stage 3. What an idiot!

I have talked about 'having a choice' before, and you do have a choice whether to take the test or not. Think of it this way: if you take the test and it comes out clear, you can celebrate; however, if you take the test and it indicates cancer, then you can also look upon that as a positive, as if you had not taken the test and had carried on as normal, it could be a much worse prognosis when it is found.

Do not get hung up on thinking, 'What if I test positive?' Believe me, you do not want this disease, and so if you are given a chance to test for it, I would take it every time. Time is of the essence; the sooner it is caught, the better for everyone.

6

Chemotherapy

Now, before I start, please remember what was said to me and what I have said: chemotherapy may affect each person in different ways, and what I experienced is not necessarily what others will experience.

What also needs to be kept in mind is that there are different treatments and different doses used to treat colon cancer; therefore, the word chemotherapy does not necessarily mean the same thing for each person. It is a drug-based anti-cancer treatment that can include numerous drugs taken singularly or in combination, in tablet or liquid form, along with a variety of treatments that may be given alongside the drug treatment.

Chemotherapy travels around your body in your bloodstream; therefore, it can reach every part of your body. The point of it is to kill cells that are dividing into two new cells.

I will freely admit that at the time I didn't fully read and digest what was written in the chemotherapy paperwork, as reading the side-effects was enough to change my mind about having it in the first place. This is unusual for me, but I thought that there was no point in reading it all and worrying about all of the possibilities that could happen; I had made my decision, and I just wanted to get started. What will be, will be.

The letter that came with the side-effects information also mentioned a long list of possible toxicities. Toxicity is the degree to which a substance is poisonous. Poisonous! This is serious medication. The letter also explained how the medication needed to be handled. 'Handled?'

The medication that I received was a combination called CAPOX, a combination of oxaliplatin and capecitabine. Oxaliplatin is a liquid that was fed intravenously straight into one of my veins via a cannula, while capecitabine came in tablet form.

My treatment was spread over a twelve-week period, which was split into four three-weekly cycles. On the first day of each cycle, I went to the hospital for a day to have the oxaliplatin administered, and then I took capecitabine tablets for two weeks whilst I was at home. The third week was a rest week to give my body time to recover before it started all over again. This cycle was repeated four times.

A reason why the treatment is split over an extended period of time is that some cancer cells can remain dormant; therefore, they may elude the chemotherapy drugs, as the drugs are looking to kill cells that are dividing into two. The hope is that at some point during treatment, the dormant or resting cancer cells will start to divide and will be killed by the chemotherapy drugs [29].

At the start of each cycle, my partner drove me to the hospital, as it was not advised to drive immediately after treatment. My first day consisted of being given a booklet containing even more information, which also had places to make notes during each cycle. I was meant to take this with me at the start of each cycle, which I duly did. There was a lot to take in, and so it was useful for me to make notes and take the information with me as a reference point as my treatment progressed. I still had to take my temperature at home and make notes of any side-effects that I was having, and there was a place to put my various blood readings too.

After I had been given my booklet, I was weighed and had my blood pressure and temperature taken. Yes, you can guess the response to my blood pressure reading – the same as usual. At least I could tell them that my GP had now been notified and that my blood pressure was going to be addressed after my treatment.

I didn't get away with it so easily this time though, as they didn't like giving treatment if your diastolic reading (the second set of numbers of your reading) was over one hundred, which mine nearly always was. This made matters worse, as I was now worried that I would be refused treatment. I lay there on a couch, desperately trying to relax to try and lower my blood pressure. It seemed to work, as I could get it down to around one hundred. Each time I was asked if I had a headache, if I had any chest pains, or if I felt unwell. Each time I answered, 'I'm fine, same as usual.'

A record of your weight is important, as you need to maintain your weight to cope with the treatment. If you start to lose weight, it could point to something being wrong, i.e., your body is not coping. Thankfully, I maintained my weight throughout. I made a point of doing so after understanding how important it was both before and after my operation.

Once I was past this stage, a blood sample was taken. This time they were checking my DPD levels (an enzyme that helps break down chemotherapy drugs), as if my DPD levels were too low and the chemotherapy drugs started to accumulate in my body, I could be at risk of developing an increased level of side-effects that could possibly be life threatening [30]. My platelets (which help blood to clot), red blood cells (which carry oxygen around your body), and white blood cells (which fight infection) were also checked.

All of these checks were carried out to make sure that I was in a fit state to cope with the treatment. If they were too low, this could result in my treatment being postponed until the numbers have risen to an acceptable level.

The one element that dropped in number throughout my treatment was my platelet count, but not enough to warrant a delay, thankfully. As all of my readings were satisfactory and within set limits, my chemotherapy was then prepared. One thing I was very wary of was catching COVID or anything else due to the treatment weakening my immune system. I was actually classified as 'vulnerable' at this point and was offered priority flu and COVID injections, which I gladly accepted.

I then got to sit in a comfy chair along with other patients and had a cannula inserted into the top of my hand. The other people could be there for any cancer; it wasn't just for colon cancer. One of the first things that I noticed was that all of the ladies were wearing bandanas or hats due to their hair either falling out or having already fallen out. This is one of the side-effects that I think most people are aware of, but women are more prone to it than men.

A man's hair is more likely to thin than to fall out completely. The hair should grow back after around six months, although it is likely to be thinner and softer than before. During my treatment, I lost a bit of hair, and it became physically thinner and softer; it wasn't noticeable to look at.

I was made to feel at home with cushions; a TV was on in the background, and I could use my phone if I so desired. As I had let all of the relevant people know about my situation, I had plenty of people to WhatsApp, telling them of my progress and what was going on. Sandwiches and drinks were offered to us all at midday, which was nice; the time soon went by.

Once I was installed, a nurse came and plugged me into a drip. The first sensation that I felt was coldness. I could feel the cold liquid travelling through my body - every part of it. Once the effect wore off, I settled down, put my trust in others, and let it happen. As usual, I watched and took notice of what was going on around me, and I was amazed at the number of checks that were carried out before the medication was given to you. When I was admitted, I was tagged, and every time I had medication given to me, I was asked my date of birth and name while they checked it against my tag and against the medication.

They were thorough with their checks - very thorough - and there was a very good reason why. If there were patients requiring different medications for different cancers, as well as different doses, then it could be catastrophic if a high dose of the strongest drug was given to a person who could only deal with a low dose of the weakest drug.

Some of the factors that are taken into account when calculating the dosage and type of medication relevant to each person are the type of cancer they have, the person's body size and BMI (body mass index), any other medical conditions they may have, whether they are taking other medications, and how they respond to treatment. The wrong dose given to the wrong person could be disastrous.

During my treatment, I mentioned to one of the nurses that I had a toothache and asked if it would be okay if I went to see my dentist. The nurse seemed a bit put out, saying that I could not now just go to the dentist; it wasn't that simple. If I were to have treatment, I would have to speak to the dentist first to tell them about the treatment that I was undergoing, as my immune system was now compromised and there could be a problem in relation to bleeding as I had been taking anticoagulants.

I remember seeing a poster relating to sepsis whilst at the

dentist the last time that I was there. If I got an infection, I could be in real trouble. There was also the risk of catching COVID, and so I decided that I would just have to manage it the best I could. One thing that I did not want to happen was for my treatment to be delayed because of a toothache.

In the end, I decided not to go, that I would eat my food using as little pressure as possible, and that I would stay away from the tooth that was giving me grief. Thankfully, I got through it okay; it was three months of careful eating though, and not something that I wanted to think about on top of everything else.

I sat there looking around and realised that I was probably the youngest there. Throughout the twelve weeks, I would say that there were just a handful of people who were around my age. After a couple of hours, the alarm went off, indicating that my medication was nearing its end. Sometimes the alarm went off because there was a blockage in the tube. The cacophony of alarms got a bit much sometimes, as all you wanted was a bit of peace and quiet.

Each visit lasted around three hours in total by the time the initial checks had been done, the medication had been prepared, the drugs had been administered, and my tablets for the following two weeks had been prepared. When finished, I would message my partner, and she would come and collect me. I left with my chemotherapy tablets along with steroid, anti-sickness, and anti-diarrhoea tablets for my first cycle.

When we got home, I took the capecitabine tablets as advised and waited for things to happen. It is important to take the tablets when and as stated, as not doing so could have an effect on their performance.

To give you an idea of their potency, you are advised to wash your hands after coming into direct contact with the tablets, and if you cannot swallow them and have to dissolve them in water, the glass that you have used must be kept separate from other crockery and washed in isolation! I wore disposable gloves to handle my tablets. I found it easier than washing my hands every time. I remember reading the instructions and saying to my partner, 'What the bloody hell is in these tablets?' Perhaps this is where the word 'toxicity' comes into play?

As the days passed by, I did start to feel a bit more tired than usual, but I still pottered about getting things done around the house and in the garden. Other than tiredness, the other well-known side-effect is tingling in the fingers, usually when touching something cold. I did feel this, especially when delving into the fridge or freezer. It wasn't really bad; it was just a bit annoying, to be honest. It certainly wasn't bad enough for me to wear gloves or not handle things from the freezer.

Something that I did notice was that when I went to the toilet (liquid or solid), a slick was left on the surface of the water, a little bit like petrol on water. I really did start to wonder what chemicals were in the tablets to create a chemical film like they did!

During the first month of treatment, I went to see the original consultant who looked after my operation because I was feeling a twinge on my right hand side where my caecum used to be. We discussed how I was feeling, and I asked how the operation went as far as they were concerned. I was told that everything had gone very smoothly and without a hitch. I was told that I don't have cancer; it has gone; it has been taken out, and my scans showed no sign of cancer anywhere else.

We discussed chemotherapy and why I was having it - it was the fact that cells had been found in one of my lymph nodes, and having chemotherapy was described as purely a 'mopping up exercise' to ensure that any rogue cells were dealt with. It was good to be told that even though cancer cells may have escaped, it is not a forgone conclusion that they will develop into a tumour, as they could die once leaving the tumour or my immune system could kill them. This made me feel a bit more positive.

All in all, the time during my first cycle went by relatively quickly, and I remember saying to my partner, 'If this is it, then I am a happy man. I can cope with this.' I was going to pay dearly for those words later on! Boy was I.

During my first cycle, I did something that I was not meant to do: I drank something cold straight out of the fridge. I was told that if I did, my throat was most likely going to snap

110

shut, just for a second, and then it would relax again. I forgot what I had been told and poured myself a nice, refreshing drink, only to have it catapulted across the kitchen as my throat reacted to the cold, snapped shut, and ejected my drink all over the kitchen floor and down my clothes! They were right, though; it did only last for a second or two as my throat relaxed back to normal.

The feeling of something happening that was out of my control was a bit scary and unnerving. The treatment made me yearn for a cold drink - something refreshing - but I could not physically drink it! This was the start of the nasty game that the drugs played on me. It seemed like they did everything they could to prevent me from getting better by hindering my food and drink intake, which was exacerbated by the fact that one evening I started hiccupping.

When I say hiccupping, I mean loudly and nonstop, well into the early hours. I woke up the next morning, and I felt okay, albeit a bit shell-shocked. Later in the day, the hiccups started again, and I thought about how I could stop them or at least reduce their strength. I knew that they came from the diaphragm, and so when I felt them coming, I held a cushion tightly against my diaphragm, and it seemed to prevent the muscle from going into spasm. It worked! I eventually perfected it by folding my arms and pressing against my diaphragm; it worked just as well.

I also practiced a method of breathing to stop them. I would inhale deeply and slowly, and when I exhaled, I would close my eyes, concentrate, and imagine that I was pushing that air back down, which meant flexing my stomach muscles and presumably my diaphragm. This also stopped the hiccups. I was well impressed with myself!

My taste had also started to change, as I woke up each morning with an awful metallic taste in my mouth. It made me salivate and feel like my jaw was a little dislocated - it was the strangest feeling. Thankfully, eating something soon got rid of it.

I would usually start the morning with a bowl of cereal, but I had to wait for the milk to warm up a little before I could eat it. I set my alarm as usual to remind me when to take my tablets. When the alarm went off, I donned disposable gloves and popped the tablets into my mouth, quickly washing them down with a drink. I washed the glass separately and threw my gloves away. While I was doing this, I was wondering what I was swallowing and what it was doing to my body. Midway through the first cycle, things that I enjoyed eating were now tasting very different, almost like burnt caramel.

Normally, as I am sure the vast majority of people do, I take eating for granted in that I go into a cupboard and find what I want to eat - something that I enjoy the taste of. Now imagine that you no longer like what you used to like because it now tastes unpleasant. Also remember that you have to keep your weight and calorie intake up to provide your body with the necessary energy and nutrition that it now requires, not just to survive but to cope with the treatment as well.

At the same time, I was desperate for a nice, cold, refreshing drink; I now couldn't have one. I know that I should be grateful that I have a nice choice of food to choose from in the first place and that it is readily available, but it makes it very difficult when what you like is no longer what you like. It now becomes very much a mental problem as well as a physical one.

When I was rummaging in the kitchen cupboards, I saw a bag of ready salted crisps. My eyes lit up; I thought something salty would be nice. After putting a few crisps in my mouth, I felt a tingling sensation. I carried on devouring the crisps, only to find that the tingling sensation was turning into a burning sensation. It felt like my mouth was on fire and was full of ulcers. Surely this could not happen, not in such a short space of time?

Not to be beaten, I finished the bag and went upstairs to look at the inside of my mouth. There were indeed blisters all around the inside of my mouth! How on earth could something like that happen so quickly? Well, I can assure you it did. Thankfully, the blisters disappeared the same day, and I hid the rest of the crisps!

When the second week of the first cycle was over, I had a week off. What a magical feeling that was! Within a couple of days, the intensity of the side-effects started to reduce, and I could drink cold, refreshing drinks again; even my taste started to return to normal. It was a marvellous feeling, like being reborn.

During my week off, I went out in the car and did the shopping. I wore a mask and gloves and sanitised throughout to keep myself from catching COVID. If I caught COVID, I would not be allowed into the hospital for my treatment, and with the possibility of catching long COVID, I was taking no risks. This was my one day out after two weeks of being stuck at home.

Other side-effects that I encountered during my first cycle were sneezing frequently in the evening, a runny nose, tiredness, twitching muscles, my right hand calf feeling tender, and sore eyes. I would say the worst of these side-effects were the twitching muscles. I could be sitting there, and muscles all over my body would twitch all by themselves. No one could see it, but it was a strange feeling.

My second cycle started exactly the same as my first, with a visit to the hospital and my temperature, blood, and blood pressure being checked. The nurse asked me how I had gotten on during my first cycle, and I replied very well. We discussed my side-effects, and I was plugged in as before.

Nothing different happened apart from me hearing about a person who had an accident while driving home after having had their chemotherapy treatment. When the police asked them where they had been, they told them about being at the hospital and having just had chemotherapy treatment. Apparently, their insurers wouldn't settle their claim because they were told that they shouldn't have been driving. The rest of the day soon passed, and it was time to call my partner so that I could be collected along with my medication.

The time in the hospital was the same, but when I got home, it certainly was not. I sat in a chair with my forearm resting on the arm of the chair as my partner sorted our tea out. After a few minutes, I shouted to my partner to come and look at my hand. My hand had not dropped; it stayed as straight as my arm, even though there was nothing underneath to support it. The muscles in the forearm that the cannula had been in had contracted. After about thirty minutes, my hand eventually dropped as the muscles began to relax. It was the strangest of feelings. I ended up having many 'strange feelings' throughout my treatment!

During the second cycle, I felt that things had changed, as the effects were more pronounced and stronger. Maybe it built up in my body the more I took of it? In bed at night, I would find myself flexing muscles all over my body as though I were stiff and aching, and the twitching of muscles became even more pronounced - even my eyelids succumbed to it.

I was really struggling with food too; it was getting so bad that I had to force myself to eat so as to maintain my body weight and strength. Not only was I suffering with my taste changing, but my tongue now felt as though I had eaten something too hot - it felt scolded.

With this in mind, I went through the contents of the fridge and the cupboards, trying everything in the hope that I could find something that tasted nice and that I enjoyed eating. I ended up eating lots of grapes, strawberries, and satsumas, along with handmade spicy sausage rolls direct from a local butcher.

My palate had changed from eating biscuits and chocolate to eating fruit and spicy sausage rolls! It is strange how my taste changed during the treatment. My second cycle ended with a week off, and I did the shopping and ventured outside in the garden more, as I could withstand the cold a little bit better during my week off.

When I went to the hospital to start my third cycle, after the usual booking in checks, I mentioned that the side-effects had been more severe during my second cycle. It was then that I found out that the medication given to me during the first cycle was a 'test' to see how I coped with it. As I had coped with it very well, the dose was increased to my 'max dose.' I did not know this - no wonder I was feeling and thinking that the side-effects were more pronounced!

The afternoon went by with me thinking about the 'stronger potion' running through my veins and how it would affect me. I sat searching the Internet in relation to the book that I was writing, and before I knew it, the alarm was going off, and it was time to be unplugged and sent home with my medication.

When I got home, I told my partner that I needed to go for a run. She looked at me gone out and asked what I was talking about, as going for a run was not the usual response that you get from someone who has just returned after having had chemotherapy.

Seconds later, I was running up the road and around the top corner. I think that my body was telling me that I had to exercise due to the buildup of toxins in my muscles. It felt good for a short while, but part of the way along the middle road, I felt tingling in my face, which soon turned to stinging and became more painful. The sensation started to spread into my nose and down the back of my throat. What I didn't account for was that it was nearly tea time and it had become pretty cold. I started to panic a little as I walked slowly back home, breathing as shallowly as I could.

What was also building up was a feeling of depression. It was always most prominent during the first three days of treatment. I first started to feel it at the start of my second cycle. As I took steroids for the first three days of each cycle, I thought they were causing my low moods, but when I spoke to the nurse about them, I was told that they help reduce the level of side-effects, so I was to keep taking them.

When I searched to find out more, I was somewhat glad that I had kept taking them, as they can assist in killing cancer cells and can increase the effectiveness of other cancer treatments; however, mood swings and depression were listed as possible side-effects [31]!

I also read about the possible side-effects of oxaliplatin, and guess what I saw? Low moods and becoming depressed [32]! It was no wonder that my head was in a mess during those first few days! The depression always started to dissipate after the third day, but the level of depression increased after every cycle. In fact, it turns out that most of my symptoms appeared to be on the list of side-effects relating to this particular drug.

While I was at home trying to eat my dinner, I broke down in tears as I struggled to do such a simple thing. When my partner came home, she could see that I was distressed, and we snuggled up on the sofa, and she held me while I wept.

During my third cycle, I was becoming quite stubborn in relation to my side-effects, as I would stand in the utility room ironing and washing completely naked with my bare feet on the cold tiles. It was as though I was making myself do it - not punishing myself, but not putting up with it or kowtowing to it anymore. Even though it was cold outside, I would go out and wash both cars. I remember once that I stayed out so long that I lost the feeling in my hands, and as I was drying the cars, my hands were just rolling over; I couldn't keep them straight. I suppose it was me sticking two fingers up at what was happening to me.

This probably was not the best thing to do, as I later read that it was best to keep the body's extremities warm so as to protect the nerves. Maybe that is why I ended up with a black mark on my wiener. It also probably explained why the nurses were very diligent in making sure that everyone was kept warm during treatment by providing blankets for everyone. I just thought they were being courteous!

It is amazing how what you think is correct can in fact be so wrong! It is almost certainly worth asking the people who know rather than applying your own logic and possibly coming up with the wrong answer. I was wrong on so many occasions, and if I had followed my own path, it could have been detrimental to my recovery.

My fourth and last cycle was, by far, the worst. Mentally and physically, I really needed it to end. I knew that there was light at the end of the tunnel, but I also knew that I had to go through the first three days, which were always the worst due to the depression and cramps.

The last cycle went as usual, and I sat there waiting for the effects of the oxaliplatin to take place. By now, the forearm that I had the cannula in was quite sore - not because of the cannula, but because that is where the oxaliplatin entered my body. I couldn't wait for it to be over and to go home.

As this was my last visit, I was given a certificate and asked if I wanted to ring the bell and have my picture taken. I am a very private person, and even though I knew I didn't have to go back, I declined and took the certificate home. One thing that I did on leaving was to thank all of the nurses in person for the care and compassion shown to me during my stays. I will be forever grateful.

It didn't take long for the side-effects to kick in as I struggled walking to the car park thanks to my leg muscles cramping up. We got home, and I could hardly walk; I was putting one foot slowly in front of the other. You wouldn't describe it as walking. This really did upset me, as it was the worst I had ever been, and I knew that the next three days would be hell if this was anything to go by.

My partner cooked me my favourite meal: a small piece of white fish and cheesy mash. Halfway through eating it, I lost control of my tongue. Your tongue is used to talk, move food around your mouth, and swallow; I couldn't do any of them. I sat there and couldn't speak as I had a mouthful of food, and tears started to run down my cheeks as I felt so useless and helpless. To make matters worse, I was also struggling to hold my knife and fork; I was that fatigued.

When my partner came in, she could see that I was in distress and sat holding my hand. After a while, when I had gained control of my tongue, enabling me to speak, I managed to explain what had just happened. By that time, we were both in floods of tears; it was so upsetting. I probably set a record for the longest time taken to eat what was on my plate. For me, it felt like a marathon.

I think I was at the end of my tether and at the end of my ability to cope with the dose that I was being given. When I say it was killing me, it could well have been. It was a nightmare.

I would say that I was at my lowest during the first week of my last cycle; it was all becoming too much. I now just had to get through my final two weeks of taking tablets, and I was finished. I will be honest, and I told my partner this later: I almost threw the final week's tablets away as I'd just had enough. Thankfully, common sense and willpower prevailed, and I did complete the course of tablets in full.

The two weeks passed, and I came out the other side. Over time, the side-effects slowly wore off, apart from the pimples and the tingly feet. Just under a year later, I still got occasional tingles in my feet and pimples on my hips, but nothing like I did whilst undergoing treatment. Occasionally, I got the odd hiccup, usually when I was preparing a meal or around food. It is a little bit like Pavlov's experiment when a dog was trained to salivate at the sound of a bell because the dog recognised being fed with the ringing of a bell. I started hiccupping when I thought of preparing a meal. How weird is that?

I really did not miss taking tablets because it seemed like my life had been ruled by them. I calculated that I had taken over six hundred tablets during my twelve weeks of chemotherapy. Six hundred!

Here is a long list of side-effects that I suffered from during my treatment:

- not being able to swallow cold drinks.
- Dry, itchy eyes.
- Constant sneezing and a runny nose.
- Involuntary twitching of muscles all over my body, even my eyelids.

- Tingling in my feet, fingers, and face when exposed to the cold. Cancer drugs or treatments can affect your nervous system by altering how your nerves function. I would think that this is probably the side-effect that most people associate with chemotherapy. The feeling can be different for each person, along with its intensity; mine lasted for nearly nine months. I found that the longer it went on, the more it faded.

  Now, nearly a year after my treatment ended, I am free from it, apart from the very occasional feeling in my feet. It is nothing more than that - just a feeling. However, like other side-effects, it can end up being permanent and may need treatment.

- A metallic taste in my mouth first thing in the morning. Once I had eaten, it tended to wear off.

- A feeling of general queasiness that I was given tablets for. I only took them when the feeling became too bad to tolerate. At no point did I think that I was going to throw up, though.

- My taste changed; the normal food that I would have eaten tasted like burnt caramel.

- Extreme hiccups: I started hiccupping early on. The first time, it lasted all evening and into the night. Later, it started whenever I thought of food or was going to eat. I found that holding a cushion tight against my diaphragm helped, and then I progressed to pressing my folded arms against my diaphragm. I also used a method of inhalation to control them.

- A flaky scalp: I had never suffered from dandruff before.
- My hair physically thinned, and I lost a little. It is okay now, just a bit finer than it was.
- During the first three days of treatment, I became very depressed; I hit rock bottom. It was awful. This was always after the first day of every cycle, when I had been given oxaliplatin intravenously and when I took steroids.
- Red pimples on my butt cheeks, hips, and shoulders. They weren't anything more than pimples. I scratched one, as I always do, and made it bleed. It was then that I noticed how different my blood was. Normally, my blood is very dark red; this was light red and looked to have clear fluid around it in some instances. It was nothing like it used to be.
- Cramp in my muscles, particularly during the night. I would constantly feel the need to flex my muscles throughout my body. Whenever I came back from my first day of treatment, I always suffered from cramps in the arm that the medication had been fed into.
- The really weird side-effect that I had was that the end of my foreskin turned brown and had a small black mark on it. Before you say anything, bearing in mind what I have said previously, I hadn't put it anywhere where it shouldn't have been! Thankfully, it returned to its normal colour over time, but the small black mark still remains!

- I found that when I went for a pee, it was not as forthcoming as it normally was; it was more of a struggle. I actually suffer from an irritable bladder, so this was an unusual feeling for me; usually it is the opposite - I am running to the loo.
- My tongue felt like it had been burnt.
- Two lumps appeared on the palm of my left hand, as well as a lump on the sole of my right foot. They are not painful as such, but I know that they are there.
- Ulcers in my mouth when eating salted crisps.
- The loss of control of my tongue while eating. Thankfully, this only happened once.

One thing that I did to celebrate after I had finished treatment was to tuck into a Belgian chocolate waffle. I had seen it sitting there in the cupboard for weeks. It took about a minute to warm up in the microwave and about the same length of time to devour it. God, it tasted good! Just a few minutes later, I was running up the stairs to evacuate the contents of my bowels. Maybe it was not such a good idea, as fatty foods are not the bowel's favourite!

To sum up my chemotherapy experience, the best way that I can describe it is 'a war of attrition' - the continual wearing down of someone until they can no longer physically fight back. For me, this is what it represented - it was punishing, gruelling, and just horrendous. Looking back on it, I remember saying to my partner that the operation was a walk in the park compared to chemotherapy and that I would rather go through two or three operations than have chemotherapy.

Not long after (around three weeks) I had finished, I booked appointments at my opticians and at my dentist. I wanted to see my dentist due to the toothache that I had, and the optician to check that my eyes were okay after having chemotherapy. Thankfully, I got my teeth sorted, and my eyes were fine.

Please remember that this was my journey and does not portray what will happen to you or others. Chemotherapy is tailored to the recipient and can be adjusted to accommodate the individual's needs even once the treatment has started.

The one thing that I have learned from my hospital experience is to do as I am told. I now also appreciate how important it is to be fit and healthy, as it can alter what surgery and treatment you have. The fitter and healthier you are, the easier it should be for you and the better your chance of recovery.

So, what are my thoughts with regards to chemotherapy? Bearing in mind a cancer cell's ability to lay dormant for years and the relatively short period of time that I had chemotherapy, I think it is a pretty blunt tool as well as being a broad-brush approach. I think there is a lot of hope invested in it.

There are a couple of expressions to be aware of. The first is that I was told that I no longer have cancer. This, to me, was what I wanted to hear, but in reality, what was being said was that my tumour had been taken out; therefore, I no longer had cancer, as in a growth or tumour. It had nothing to do with the fact that I could still have cancer cells circulating in my body, which, at some stage, could turn into a tumour.

The other expression is chemotherapy being called a mopping-up exercise. This broadly means the treatment will kill any remaining cancer cells that may have escaped.

Bearing in mind the longevity of a cancer cell and the short period of time that my chemotherapy took place, I think I would be very lucky not to have secondary cancer at some stage. Very lucky indeed!

Maybe the chemotherapy should be spread out over a longer period of time, or a second round of a lesser dose administered at a later stage, perhaps six or twelve months on? Maybe this takes place every twelve months for three years? I don't know, but I think it would be worth looking at, especially as chemotherapy is now being used in different ways, e.g., to shrink the tumour before the operation. Food for thought!

7

Where I am now

Well, it has now been around sixteen months since I had my operation, and I am feeling well. I had a CT scan after chemotherapy, which was clear again, although I felt so sorry for the guys who did my scan that day.

I arrived for the scan at eight o'clock in the morning for an eight-thirty appointment. I arrived early, as the scanner was located outside of the hospital. I eventually found it, but there was no sign of anyone. After about fifteen minutes, I called the hospital to make sure that I had the correct time and the correct location, and I was assured that someone would be there soon. A few minutes later, someone else arrived. I asked them if they were having a CT scan, to which they replied that they were.

A nurse arrived as we were talking and said that they would not be long as it took time for the scanner to be made ready. It turned out that whoever had booked the appointments had started booking them half an hour before the scanner was ready and had booked them at fifteen-minute intervals instead of every thirty minutes. Oops! They were in for a hell of a day!

Investigation-wise, I will have another CT scan when I hit the three-year mark, and I will have another colonoscopy in five months' time. This will be the penultimate physical check, as I will have, hopefully, my final colonoscopy at the end of the five-year term. In between, I will have blood tests around every six months to check my CEA markers, etc.

My CEA markers throughout my journey are as follows:

Two months before my operation - 2.7.
Ten days before my operation - 2.9.
Three weeks after my operation - 1.7.
Twelve weeks after my operation - 1.8.
Fifteen weeks after my operation - 2.3.
Eighteen weeks after my operation - 2.6.
Twenty-four weeks after my operation - 2.6.
Thirty-seven weeks after my operation - 2.7.
Forty-nine weeks after my operation - 3.0.

So, what do my results mean? It means that they are below the median number of 3.4, which is good. On the other hand, they have been increasing ever since my operation, which, looking at it singularly, does not look so good. Maybe they will settle around the median number. Time will tell.

When I had my second cystoscopy, I was talking to the nurse about markers, as my PSA markers were under investigation in relation to my prostate. I mentioned the fact that my CEA markers were well within normal limits less than two weeks before my operation. I said that I would have thought that they would be sky high, bearing in mind when they were taken. The nurse said something along the lines of, 'Imagine what state you would have been in if nothing had been done until your markers had reached what is deemed to be a dangerous level?'

They were quite right; if my markers had been the only method of investigation, then nothing would have been done, as they did not indicate a raised CEA level. Maybe my markers will settle at an acceptable level; I don't know. What I do know is that, judging by the above, markers are not the be-all and end-all; they are a part of the bigger picture. I suppose I will just have to wait until my next blood test in just over eight weeks to see if they have increased anymore.

Having said that, my CT scans have all been clear. The negative for me in all of this is the finding of a cancer cell(s) in a nearby lymph node. Have any cancer cells survived chemotherapy and started to cause problems elsewhere? All I can do is keep my fingers crossed that none did escape and survive and to get on with my life the best I can.

It is said that if you have had bowel cancer, there is an increased risk of getting it again, or that there is a slightly increased risk of getting bowel cancer if you have had another form of cancer. Family history can also affect your chances of developing bowel cancer, as if you have had a first-degree relative such as a parent, brother, sister, son, or daughter develop bowel cancer, this will increase your risk of developing it. The risk will increase further should more than one relative be diagnosed with it or if a first-degree relative develops bowel cancer at an early age - 45 or less [33].

I will just have to keep my fingers crossed and hope that I remain clear.

Something I promised that I would do after it was all over was visit the nurses who looked after me throughout my journey and deliver flowers to them all. Due to COVID, I called beforehand to make sure that I could visit rather than just turn up unannounced. Having been given the thumbs up, I went off to the supermarket and literally filled a trolley with bouquets of flowers - over twenty of them.

The funniest thing was that when I turned up at the chemotherapy unit, someone shouted, 'The man with the flowers is here!' I gave the nurses the flowers along with a card thanking everyone for being so kind and patient and for the care that they had all shown to me, a stranger. The sad thing was their response - that no one had ever bought them flowers before.

While trying to find the consultant and their secretary (who helped me on a number of occasions) at the hospital where I had my operation, I got a bit lost and ended up calling them from the car park. They asked me where I was, and I said, 'Probably not where I want to be seen to be. I am somewhere between sexual diseases and maternity!' Thankfully, they came and rescued me.

For me, this was the least that I could do. I send a Christmas card each year to the consultant, saying that I am still here and thanking them for that. I also dropped off flowers for the colorectal nurses and for nurses at the ward where I spent five days recovering after my operation. My heartfelt thanks to them all.

When it was all finished, I had a face-to-face review meeting with a colorectal nurse. We discussed my bowel habits, and I commented that they had been marvellous before my chemotherapy had started, but as soon as I started my treatment, my bowel habits changed.

It was unfortunate that at the same time I started my treatment, I could also expand my diet to whatever I fancied. My three months of a restricted diet were up; therefore, there were a number of things that had changed at the same time, including the effect that chemotherapy had on me, which could have affected my bowel habits.

What happened was that instead of my stools being firm, they were softer - it was a little bit like squeezing toothpaste, but not quite as soft. When I went to the loo, I also had to have the window open, as now a very unpleasant smell was emitted. This really worried me, as the only symptom that I could think of that linked me to cancer was a change in my bowel habits.

We spoke of this, and she told me to bear in mind that my gut had not been altered or tampered with for over fifty years, and then all of a sudden it has cancer to deal with; it gets flushed out and inflated numerous times along with scopes being inserted into it; it stops functioning completely for the first time, and then a part of it is cut away and it is sewn back together shorter than it was. It is therefore not going to be a happy bunny when it wakes up again to then have its diet altered again and further treatment such as chemotherapy. I was told that it was not uncommon to have softer stools.

One of the many side-effects of the chemotherapy was diarrhoea; therefore, even though I didn't have diarrhoea, this, along with the change to my diet, could well explain the softness of my stools. At the end of the day, my bowel is going to take time to get back into a rhythm, and things will more than likely be different from the way they were. I asked if I would need to eat more due to my bowel being shorter and was told that this was a common question and that I did not need to eat more to compensate for its reduction in length.

The nurse asked about any side-effects that I had been left with from the chemotherapy. I said that my muscles were still a bit cramped; I got hiccups, but nothing like when I was having treatment; the red pimples came and went around my hips; my feet were still a bit tingly and could get sore if I walked a distance; and that I had a flaky scalp now, which I did not have before.

On asking what the future was relating to care, I was told that I was on a five-year plan and that I would have another CT scan in sixteen months and hopefully my final colonoscopy at the end of the five years, riddled with blood tests in between to monitor my CEA markers. That was all of my questions answered, so I thanked her and her team for their patience, care, and understanding and for doing what they do: answering our questions during a very difficult time, looking after us, and putting our minds at rest. I have nothing but the highest regard for these people; they really are angels.

Throughout my treatment, I still received calls from the colorectal nurses asking me if everything was still okay or if there was anything that I wanted to discuss. After my chemotherapy had finished, I mentioned the initial meeting with the chemotherapy consultant and how upsetting it was to one of the colorectal nurses, as my partner had been reduced to tears during the meeting. I was told that I could register a complaint and that if I wasn't happy with the way that we had been treated, then I should make a complaint.

I also said that I had no follow-up meeting after the chemotherapy treatment had finished, just a letter that I could take in different ways due to the terminology used. I said that I would have thought that even a ten-minute meeting to confirm that everything was okay and to answer any questions would have been a minimum requirement for someone who had been through what I had been through. The nurse agreed with me, saying that it wasn't acceptable and that she would send an email immediately. I liked this nurse. There was no messing with her.

Not long after, I received notification that an appointment with the consultant had been arranged! Even this was a bit of a cockup. I arrived early again, and out of courtesy, I turned my phone off. The time went by again, and so I asked at reception if I should book in for the meeting or whether I should just wait; they checked the computer and told me to just wait. More time went by, and the receptionist noticed me still standing there and rang through to the consultant. A couple of minutes later, I was ushered in.

The consultant said that they had tried to call me on several occasions. I told them that my phone was turned off and that surely the receptionist, when checking, should have noticed and told me that it was in fact a telephone meeting that had been booked. They agreed and commented that things were not working as well as they should in certain areas.

The meeting was thankfully more amiable than the first, and they confirmed that everything had gone well and that my last CEA reading was within normal range, so I was going to be discharged from oncology and that I would be handed back to the follow-up colorectal team. That was all I wanted to hear!

One thing that I did mention was my stools being soft and how they had changed since my operation. I explained that I was worried that this could be a sign of my cancer returning. My mind was put at ease when they explained that my CT scan was clear and that this cancer doesn't happen that quickly. We talked for a while about how I had coped and any side-effects that I had.

While I had their attention, I asked how the NHS was going to cope with the ratio now put at one in two people developing cancer in their lifetime [34]. That is half the population! It is not as though cancer specialists grow on trees, whether they are nurses or consultants. I was given a shrug of the shoulders and the answer that they really weren't sure what was going to happen. I thanked them and wished them well.

Thanks to a letter from one of the nurses to my GP, my blood pressure was addressed. I was duly sent a blood pressure form to complete, so I decided to buy a blood pressure monitor off the Internet, enabling me to check it myself while at home. I waited a couple of months, at least, before I took any readings to enable my body to get back to a near-normal state. During this time, I went to see the nurse at my GP to compare the readings of my blood pressure monitor against theirs. I took readings for about three weeks and sent the readings to my GP.

A week or so later, I received a call from my GP, who suggested that I try some tablets to help bring it down. I agreed to this on the proviso that if I wanted to come off them for any reason, I could do so without incurring any side-effects. This was agreed upon, and I went to collect them. Months later, my blood pressure has dropped to 148/86, somewhat better than before and with no side-effects.

The time soon came for my next routine colonoscopy. I received the medication (laxatives) and knew what I had to do only too well. On the day, having tested clear of COVID, I arrived and got booked in. A cannula was inserted into my vein, and I was taken on a trolley to the appropriate room. There were just two people this time: one who had put my cannula in and an endoscopist who I could not understand. I mentioned having gas when I needed it, as the apparatus was still against the wall and not near me. I mentioned again that I would need it and was told that they would bring it to me if I needed it.

After a few minutes, I was getting bad cramps and, funnily enough, asked for the gas, which was brought to me. I inhaled and felt nothing - no reduction in pain. The scope was inserted further, and I was in agony. I inhaled as much as I could, and still nothing - no dulling of the senses.

It was explained to me that due to my colon being shorter, the two corners were now much tighter; therefore, there was less room to manoeuvre. This went on for what felt like an eternity, and I was asked if I would rather stop and come back another time, to which I replied categorically, 'No, I want to get it done!' There was no way that I was quitting and having to come back again.

Near the end, I think I passed out briefly, as I was in so much pain. The only thing that I can conclude from this is that either the gas had not been turned on, there was no gas in the cylinder, or the apparatus was faulty. Whatever it was, it was an unpleasant and painful experience.

At the end of the session, I was told that whoever carried out my surgery was very good, as the joint was hardly noticeable.

What I wanted to hear - that I was clear - was also confirmed, and I was congratulated on having a very healthy bowel. Although it was a bad experience in relation to the lack of pain relief, I was over the moon with the results: nothing was found.

I received the report not long after, along with the photographs, and was delighted - everything was normal. One of the photographs was even taken inside the small colon; they went that far in.

In relation to the physical aspect of what had happened to me, that was pretty much it. I had another CT scan and a final colonoscopy booked for the future; I felt fine, and my wounds were barely noticeable, so I wasn't thinking about any of that.

The one thing that I can say and that I still feel is strange is that throughout my cancer's development and during my operation and chemotherapy, I never suffered from pain, apart from my first cystoscopy and my last colonoscopy. I wouldn't say the chemotherapy was painful; it is difficult to explain – debilitating, depressing, tiring, frustrating, but not painful. I have previously suffered pain due to a broken wrist and a compressed tendon, and so I was grateful that this journey came without it.

The mental side, however, was a different story. Even though I had been given the all clear through numerous tests, I was still plagued with the thought that something had nearly killed me - something that I didn't even know was there!

This made me think about any slight change in my body and its functions. I found myself going to see my GP and asking them to look at a lump on my cheek. It wasn't causing me any discomfort and had been there for years. I had put it down to a lump of fatty tissue, which the doctor did too. I was told that if it became painful or changed in any way, I should make another appointment to see them.

While I was there, we also discussed my co-morbidities: a cyst on one of my epididymides (a tube attached to each testicle) and a polyp in my gallbladder. I was reassured that the cyst was just a sac filled with fluid and maybe sperm, and that this and the polyp should be harmless and not malignant (cancerous).

Even though my GP had assured me that there was nothing wrong, I still went ahead and booked an appointment at a private clinic for a testicular scan. I drove to Leeds to meet the lady who was going to perform my scan. On arrival, I was asked if I needed a chaperone. I had not been asked this before and so said, 'No thanks, I trust you.' I was duly stared at like I was a naughty boy!

The scan went well, and I asked her about the cyst that I was told I had. It turned out that I had two, one in either side of my scrotum, and they were no danger to me. A couple of my tubes were blocked, and that could be a reason for the cysts forming; they were only a couple of millimetres in size.

I searched on the Internet, and it said that such cysts can cause an aching sensation, which was the reason that I was having the scan. I left my self-diagnosis and my anxiety at that.

I did, however, have a 'wobble' around twelve months after my chemotherapy. It started when I felt a stinging sensation when I peed on Tuesday; on Wednesday it was still stinging and my temperature had increased to 38.8°C, and I was peeing very frequently; on Thursday I started to lose control of my bladder in that I had very little time to get to the toilet before I wet myself, and my temperature had increased to 39°C.

Just to add to the fun that I was having, I started peeing out of my bottom too, just like when I took the laxative the day before I had a colonoscopy. I called my GP on Friday as I thought that I had passed blood in my pee and was now petrified that the cancer had returned. After a quick consultation, I was sent to the hospital, where I needed to ask for what I thought was Aztec!

On arriving at the hospital, I went to the main reception and asked for Aztec. They didn't know what I was talking about, so I mentioned that it allowed me to bypass A&E. I was then sent to A&E, where I asked for Aztec. They looked puzzled, asking me if I meant SDEC. I said that it sounded right and went to SDEC, which turned out to stand for Same Day Emergency Care.

I explained who I was and was assigned a nurse; they knew who I was and were ready for me. Within twenty minutes, I had an ECG, my blood pressure, and my pulse taken, along with two blood samples. The nurse explained that it was most likely a UTI (urinary tract infection); I then sat waiting for the results.

After an hour or so, I got the results from the blood test that looked for infections, and a nurse confirmed that I did indeed have an infection. It was actually described as a 'raging' infection. I felt much better hearing this, as it meant that my symptoms were most likely caused by an infection rather than cancer. It is probably the only time that you are grateful to be told that you have a raging infection! I was given a prescription and sent straight to the pharmacy for some strong antibiotics.

On Monday, I went back to find out the results from my blood test relating to cancer markers. I thought that I was being tested just for bowel cancer. This is where the confusion set in, as in fact, I had been tested for both CEA (colon) and PSA (prostate) markers. As I said before, my CEA markers had been slowly increasing and were showing 3 on my last blood test, which was already worrying me. The result relating to my PSA markers was 23.7 and 4 for my CEA markers, which sent me into an immediate panic on both counts.

I had previously been given the option of having a CT scan, but I said that I would prefer to get the blood test results back first, as I knew that there was a risk, albeit a small risk, in having too many. However, once we had the results back on Monday, we were both in agreement that I should have a scan of the prostate area as soon as possible; therefore, I was put at the front of the queue on Tuesday's schedule.

I had been asked to arrive early so that the nurse in SDEC could fit a cannula to save the CT department time. It was at this point that a trainee nurse was involved, and I was asked if I minded that she put the cannula in. I said that I didn't mind and that everyone had to learn. I then thanked her for being a trainee, as without people like her, we would all be in trouble. She did a great job, and she came with me to watch me have my scan. It was over in ten minutes, and I was allowed to go.

Later that week, I received a call to tell me that my scan was clear and that there was no sign of metastasis - the spread of cancer from the first location. There was, however, a note saying that there was some calcification of the prostate. I searched it on the Internet, as I do, and numerous reasons for calcification came up. Some were saying that it is linked to cancer, and some were saying the opposite.

I did my usual thing and bought a dozen or more bouquets to take to the nurses, who did not know me but had looked after me. As I left, a nurse shouted, 'Excuse me, are you married?' I turned around somewhat embarrassed as another shouted, 'I bet he is; he must be; no single man does that.' I made a hasty retreat as laughter broke out in the waiting area. I don't understand why you wouldn't thank someone who has helped you in such a way, and yet I am told that they don't get given flowers.

The Monday after, I called a colorectal nurse and brought her up to speed. The interesting thing was that although I am still under their wing in relation to colon cancer, they have nothing to do with prostate cancer, even if I had it. I also mentioned the calcification of my prostate, and I was told not to worry as many organs can suffer from this.

As a part of my five-year surveillance, I am due another CEA blood test in a month and assumed that my PSA markers would be tested at the same time, but it is in fact just for my CEA markers. Always ask and never assume!

I am pleased to say that two weeks later I felt much better, especially as I had control of all of my orifices again! Walking around with your pants stuffed full of tissues is no fun!

About three weeks after this, I received an unexpected call from urology due to my visit to SDEC. Urology specialises in kidney, bladder, prostate, ureter, and reproductive organ problems. I was asked to give another blood sample, which I arranged to be taken at the same time as my planned CEA sample, and was offered an MRI scan as I was told that MRI produces clearer, better-quality images.

We agreed that the best course of action was to see what the results of the blood test were so that they could be compared to my blood test that was taken during my infection. I am pleased to say that my PSA marker dropped from 23.7 down to 9.1.

However, I was told that a reading of 9.1 is still high for my age, and so I will have another blood test in four weeks to see if it has come down any further. On delving through previous paperwork, I found a document saying that a reading of no more than 6 would be an acceptable PSA level for me.

During these four weeks, I have been asked to drink between two and three litres of water every day, right up until the date of my cystoscopy, to help clear any residual infection that might still be lingering. I may also have an internal examination and a biopsy of my prostate. Oh, what fun! More prodding, peeing, and poking about! The thought of a biopsy worried me, as just having one can lead to problems.

Not long after, I received a letter confirming that I had also been put forward for another cystoscopy due to possible blood in my pee.

To have the cystoscopy, I had to travel thirty miles in the other direction to a different hospital; I would have been to all of the hospitals within a thirty mile radius of where I live soon. It was a nice small hospital with good parking, which is always a bonus. I arrived early, sat down, and was asked the usual questions while having a blood pressure test. When the nurse read the results, she said, 'You are glad to be here then?' laughing, as my readings were high.

Once we had gone through what was going to happen, I was taken to a changing room to get undressed. The nurse came back and tagged me and told me that a lady was going to carry out the procedure, to which I asked, 'Is she in a good mood?'

I was really worried leading up to the examination, as I didn't fancy the pain that I experienced before when I tried to pee after the procedure. When I laid down, I explained my previous experience and said, 'Be gentle with me.' I do not think as much anaesthetic was applied this time, as I could feel the scope travelling down my urethra, whereas I couldn't before.

My bladder was inflated by fluid injected by the scope, so that all of the inside was visible. I am pleased to say that everything was okay, and even more pleased that I wasn't in agony when I went for a pee while getting dressed. It was such a relief on both counts - not being in agony and having no sign of cancer.

While the scope was in there, my prostate was looked at. It had red specks on it, which I assume were to do with its calcification, and I was told that it was on the large side as it was pushing against my bladder. I was also told to carry on drinking lots of water to prevent and flush out any infection as a 'foreign body' (the scope) had entered my body. I left thanking them for looking after me and now await a call from the consultant to discuss the results of my PSA blood test, the results of the cystoscopy, and the way forward. I will be going back with flowers as a thank you for their care.

I received a phone call from the consultant via a pre-booked appointment, and they confirmed that my PSA had dropped even further from 9.1 to 4.7, which was very encouraging. My pee samples were negative, showing no infection, which was more good news, and my bladder and urethra were fine.

I asked what a normal PSA reading should be and was told three or less. They went on to explain that because my prostate was slightly larger than normal, it was not a surprise that my markers were slightly elevated, as the larger it is, the more proteins it produces, which will increase your markers.

The thing is that, as far as I can remember, my prostate has always been said to be slightly larger than normal, so I am hoping that this is the only cause of my elevated markers.

At the same time as my PSA markers had dropped, so had my CEA markers – down to 2.6. This was great news, but also very confusing, as my markers had gone from 3 to 4 and are now down to 2.6. Perhaps it had to do with the infection.

With this in mind, they still wanted to investigate further to ensure that there was nothing else responsible for my prostate being larger than it should be, which left us with an MRI scan or a biopsy of my prostate. I know that I have previously steered away from having an MRI, but now I think it makes sense to have one. If something untoward is found, then I will have a biopsy. I have gone from being a person who never needed to go to a hospital to a person who now frequents them regularly.

Not long after, a letter arrived from a different consultant requesting that I meet them at the same hospital. It was a little unnerving, as there was no reason given for the meeting. I started searching for prostate biopsies and got myself wound up reading about the things that could go wrong. It is not a pleasant procedure and can have short-term as well as long-term side-effects, one of which is impotence.

The day arrived, and my partner drove me to the hospital. The consultant was very nice; we discussed what had happened to date, and they explained the reason for the meeting: to decide the way forward. I was given a rectal examination to feel my prostate, and they agreed that it was a little large but not problematic. I then turned over, and they examined my wiener, to which they said, 'Oh.'

On hearing this exclamation, I looked down and was told that my meatus (the hole I pee out of) was half the size that it should be. This could cause a problem due to insufficient pee being expelled when I go to the toilet, which leaves pee in my bladder, which could lead to infection. I was then told that they would like to carry out another cystoscopy in person and that I would be taught how to widen my urethra, which entailed sticking a dilating catheter down it! Having an MRI was now out of the window. It is funny how things can change so quickly.

The funny thing was that when I messaged a friend who was equally going through the wars, he told me that he'd had it done too and laughed relating to the insertion of the catheter! Their parting words were, 'Enjoy, but not too much!'

With regards to water, all joking aside, my kidneys used to be fit to burst if I drank half a litre of it, let alone litres of it. By water, I mean just water, not drinks containing water such as tea, coffee, or squash. Now that I am drinking it every day, my body has adapted to it, and I can hold much more water than I used to, which is a good thing as we know that water is good for the body. Not only is it good for the bowel, but it is also good for the bladder, as it helps clean it. With this in mind, I will continue to make sure that I drink a couple of litres a day on top of my teas and coffees.

Just to confirm how bad my paranoia is, I have collated a list of symptoms and booked an appointment with my GP to discuss a mole that has bled, changed colour, developed a crust around it, and another that has just changed colour. My list also includes a persistent cough, fatigue, shortness of breath, the two lumps on my hand, and tinnitus. When you read about some of the symptoms of cancer, you will understand why I did this. The thing is, we are told to go to our GP if we have some of these symptoms, but I still feel as though I am wasting their time.

I did go to my GP, who was excellent. I wrote them an email

first, telling them of my symptoms and how I was feeling, and I was told to take a pee sample in and to make an appointment to see them, which I duly did.

During my appointment, they made notes as I went down my list, and we agreed that I would go my own way in relation to tinnitus (I would contact a private specialist), that I should contact my GP should the lumps on my palm get larger or become painful, and that they would review the rest of my symptoms. Within hours, I received a message requesting that I send a photograph of the mole in question, which I duly did.

It turned out that the photograph was not good enough; therefore, I had to book a face-to-face appointment with the dermatologist. Within a few days, I was sitting in front of the dermatologist, having my mole inspected along with the moles on my back. All were said to be okay, apart from the one in question, where something had changed. I was assured that if it was a form of cancer, it was not one that could spread or cause me problems. If it turned out to be cancerous, then it could easily be taken off using laser surgery, and that would be the end of it.

Within three days, I received a message from the dermatologist confirming that the change that had taken place in relation to my mole was not anything to worry about; therefore, no further action was required. Great news and worth doing.

I feel as though I am falling apart, especially as I had to visit my GP again due to a swollen lump on my elbow (elbow bursitis), which had been caused by overwork or leaning on my elbows. When I visited again to discuss my elbow, I said that I should have my own personal chair in the waiting room with my name on it; I am there that often, especially as I am now going to have to go for an x-ray of my elbow! My mum was so right – it is no fun getting old, and she was over a decade older than me when she said it!

I genuinely find it difficult to let go of it, even though I have been given the all clear for cancer. However, what did help was talking about it. I went from not wanting to discuss it in the early stages to then wanting to discuss it and to tell people what I had been through and what I had to endure during the latter stages. I would say that I now actually enjoy talking about it; it is as though I want to talk about it to release that pent-up angst from all those months of anxiety and keeping quiet about it.

The problem that I have is that my angst is not going away, bearing in mind my most recent blood test results and the symptoms just listed. I got quite depressed at one point as I was thinking too much, trying to solve the puzzle and come up with a definitive answer, which obviously I can't. Maybe it is because of my persona - being a control freak and wanting everything to be black or white.

I have talked with other cancer sufferers about how they felt after they had been discharged, and we all said the same thing: that it leaves you with a haunted feeling, as though you are always looking over your shoulder.

As I had no symptoms, this haunted feeling was very strong in me, as I had no idea that anything was wrong in the first place. For all I know, I could still have cancer cells in me waiting to become active and start multiplying. Most of the time I am okay; I can deal with it, but every now and then a feeling of emptiness comes back, a hollow feeling.

I have been having twitches around where my caecum was, and at one point it felt like a strong pulse was also emanating from the same region. I did speak with a colorectal nurse about it but was assured that it is not uncommon to have such feelings in the region where an operation has previously taken place.

Not wanting to go to my GP again, I looked into having a full-body MRI scan carried out privately, which can cost around £1,500-£1,800 depending upon where you go and what the scan consists of, but I was put off by people saying that it is highly doubtful that it would come back so quick. I wish I had listened to myself!

I am pretty sure that I will have one done at some point, as I will be waiting another couple of years before I have a colonoscopy, and let's face it, my CEA markers don't seem to be a particularly accurate way of monitoring for colon cancer. I suppose I am erring on the side of caution too, particularly in relation to metastasis, which worries me greatly.

Cancer is incredibly difficult to put into a box, as it is reliant on so many factors and can trick your body as well as those trying to diagnose it. It is almost as though you have to have it to confirm that you have it, and of course by then it is too late.

People's responses are interesting, as some feel uncomfortable talking about it. Whether this is because they have experienced it, someone they know has experienced it, or it is something that worries them, I don't know. I even know of one person who went to a party and was told not to talk about it! I know if that was said to me, there would have been some harsh, blunt words spoken!

After my visit to have my testicles scanned, I dropped in to see an old customer who was more like a friend. After the initial greetings, I was asked how I had been and how retirement was treating me. I told them of my recent experience, and they were interested to hear all that had gone on. It was a relief to get it out of my system, and it was nice to see some old friends too.

I have seen other people who I used to work with, and it was nice to share my experience with them too, as they had known about what was happening through texts and WhatsApp, but we hadn't had time to sit down and chat about it properly over a coffee and a biscuit.

I have not had a negative response from anyone when I have spoken about it; if anything, they have asked lots of questions and have been interested in hearing about my experience. More often than not, they also have a story to tell about a colleague, a friend, or a family member who has had some form of cancer.

People have used the words 'courageous' and 'brave' when relating to what I had been through. I wouldn't call it either of those; as far as I am concerned, I just had to suck it up and get on with it. I really didn't have a choice if I wanted to stay alive. Believe me, if I did have a choice, I would rather not have had it in the first place.

Over sixteen months later, I feel okay, apart from the recent wobble. I do, however, get tired much more easily than I used to, and my feet get sore, but other than that, I physically feel no different. What lies ahead? I have no idea, and I try not to think about it. All I know is that so far, I have been given the all clear; my consultant and the colorectal team are happy with the end result and with my progress, and that I am looking forward to our next holiday and to my future with my partner.

I know that I have future examinations planned and that they are not pleasant, but what I also know and understand is that if there is something there, then it is better to tackle it sooner rather than later. I am determined to be sitting with my partner on a bench by the sea in our dotage, still enjoying our time together. What more can one ask?

8

Metastasis or not?

Three years after my diagnosis, and having thought that I had completed this book, it looks like I will be adding another few chapters! Has metastasis occurred or not? That is the million-dollar question. Let me explain.

As you will have read, I have had a few 'wobbles' along the way in relation to my health, all of which have turned out to be okay, i.e., not cancer related, but now I have a major wobble that could well be cancer related. I hope it isn't, obviously, but at the time of writing, I don't have an answer. Did I have any symptoms? I will admit to being tired, but I had been working hard for months and hadn't been sleeping well for some time. Would I relate that to having secondary cancer, also known as stage 4 cancer? Not really, no.

Six months ago, I had my regular blood test, which gave a CEA reading of 2.9, and the one six months prior to that was 2.6, so all was well. I went for my most recent blood test (three years) and waited for a phone call to let me know the result. After twelve days, I had received no follow-up phone call, so I decided to give the colorectal nurses a call to find out what my marker reading was. I was told that after thirty months, follow-up phone calls would become more infrequent, which was a surprise to me. I suppose this ties in with what I was told: that the risk of developing secondary cancer lessens the longer the time lapses after having had primary cancer.

After a couple of minutes, there was an expression of, 'Oh,' which was rather worrying. I was then told that my CEA marker had risen from 2.9 to 7.9 in the past six months, so it had nearly trebled. My immediate response was one of panic, as you can imagine. The nurse quickly called the x-ray department so that I could have an emergency CT scan and booked me another blood test for the next day.

Not long after the phone call, I did ask myself the following questions: What if I hadn't called? What if I had just left it until my next blood test and scan in six months' time? Would my results have been looked at in the interim? I have said it before and I will say it again: It pays to have an interest in your health and to not just leave it to others. I do not know if my results would have been looked at in time, but what I do know is that I am glad that I chased them up.

When I went to collect my blood test form early in the morning, it should have been for a kidney function test as well as a CEA marker test. When I looked at it, it only had the kidney check on it, which could have meant a wasted journey for me, wasted time having taken an appointment up to then have to book another one, and a delay in getting my results.

I was disappointed at how things were progressing, as things seemed to be slipping. The result from my blood test came out at 7.9 again.

The earliest CT scan that I could get booked in for was at a different hospital, nearly forty miles away. The irony was that my partner and I were attending the funeral of an old school friend earlier that day who had died of cancer! Unfortunately, I had not kept in touch, but I had seen him a couple of times at social gatherings. I remember him as a gentle guy, a genuine, nice person. Standing there during the service brought the finality of it all crashing home. It was an uncomfortable experience for me, even more so than normal, especially as we had not told anyone yet.

It was shortly after this that we decided it would be a good idea to tell friends and family and to keep them in the loop as to what was going on.

The CT scan was as usual, no problem; I just had to wait for the results. Unfortunately, the scan had picked up something on my liver, a lesion. A lesion is an abnormal growth that can be cancerous or benign. My concern is that the liver is one of the places where metastasis can occur. The lesion had not shown up on my scan six months ago, so despite people saying, 'It doesn't happen that fast,' it can!

Because I had raised markers as well as a lesion on my liver, I was booked in for an urgent MRI (magnetic resonance imaging) scan, which I had never had before; they had always been CT or ultrasound scans. As radiation is not involved in the imaging process (magnetic fields and radio waves are used to produce an image), there is no risk of radiation with an MRI scan.

When I say urgent, I was booked in at my local hospital before the department even opened its doors in the morning! Don't get me wrong, I am grateful for the speed of response and would have turned up at whatever time they wanted me to.

While all of this was happening, my medical papers were being distributed to a liver specialist and to an MDT meeting, where I would be discussed and assessed.

After the various checks had been carried out, I got changed into a robe with just my underwear and socks left on. As per my CT scan, I had a cannula inserted into my arm to enable the introduction of dye. I had heard about MRI scans before and had prepared myself for being put in a tube and the feeling of claustrophobia that it can cause. My plan was to keep my eyes closed and not touch the sides. That way, there was nothing telling me that I was encased in a tube; I could have been in a field for all I knew.

I can imagine that if you had your eyes open and saw the inside of the tube just a few inches away from your face, it could quite easily induce panic. There was, however, a nice cool stream of air flowing over my face that helped the feeling of being outside in the fresh air.

The same goes for movement. If you tried to move, say you had an itch, and you felt the solid tube around you, it could induce panic; therefore, the best solution, in my mind, was to lay completely still with my eyes closed and think that I was outside.

The process was explained to me, and that I could be in there for as long as thirty to forty minutes. I had some headphones put on me, along with a panic button placed in the palm of my hand should it become too much for me. A large, heavy pad was placed across my abdomen, which I was told would be responsible for producing the images.

I had heard that it was noisy, but I was not prepared for how loud it actually was and the vibration that came with it. The operators talked to me via the headphones and let me know what was going to happen and when, as well as giving me instructions.

For every image taken, I had to hold my breath, sometimes for quite a long period of time. I was nearly caught out a couple of times, as I couldn't hold my breath for much longer. While I was holding my breath, not moving, and keeping my eyes closed during the imaging process, there was a lot of noise and vibration, which could be constant or in pulses.

When it had finished, I got dressed and headed out to the car park. Little did I know the effect the scanner had on me, as I became quite dizzy and ended up walking across the car park sideways, heading towards my partner, who was waiting for me.

The only thing left now was to attend a meeting a few days later to discuss the results of the MRI and the way forward. If you remember earlier on, when I met the consultant who looked after my initial operation, I liked to form a connection with them; unfortunately, this was not going to happen this time around, which left me feeling a little uncomfortable.

The meeting took place in a small room with several nurses, the surgeon, and my partner and I in it. The surgeon spent a lot of time looking at the MRI images and asked me a couple of questions relating to the dates of scans that I'd had and what I knew or had been told. I hadn't, in fact, been told a great deal other than there was something on my liver – a lesion.

Unfortunately, there was very little eye contact or general discussion, as I think a part of the problem was that the consultant had only just received the MRI images and was busy looking at them and deciding what was the best course of action whilst I was sitting next to him. I had thankfully read about various options available so that I was prepared for the meeting in the hope of discussing them, but we didn't get that far.

I sat confused as I was told that the best course of action was to remove the part of my liver containing the lesion; this is called a resection. This was known to me, and as far as I understood, it was the best course of action to eradicate cancer from my liver. Remember that we are talking about secondary cancer now, not primary cancer.

I say confused, as it hadn't yet been confirmed as cancer. It was said that it was most likely to be, as the liver is one of the locations for colon cancer metastasis to occur, and I suppose when your markers have also nearly trebled, this pushes the conclusion towards metastasis having taken place.

I was given some leaflets to take away and read, and I was told that it could be four to six weeks before surgery could be performed as various meetings had to take place beforehand.

I also had to attend pre-op meetings, as I did for my first operation, to make sure that I was fit enough to cope with the surgery. I said that I just wanted it out of me as soon as possible, to which they replied that I could have the operation in a few days, but it is the pre-op that is holding the date of surgery up. This surprised me.

I admit to being a little overwhelmed by it all. It was very different compared to the meeting I had relating to my first operation, but then the circumstances were very different. I signed a consent form agreeing to the surgery as well as agreeing to a blood transfusion should it be needed. We both left in a bit of a daze, somewhat shell-shocked by it all.

This was all very upsetting for both of us. We thought that we had left this behind us, but here we were again. I said to my partner, 'I feel like I am now just an observer.' She asked what I meant, and I replied, 'It is like watching the world turn in slow motion with everyone dashing about getting on with their lives whilst I am standing at the side watching, not taking part. I no longer feel a part of it.' That feeling of loneliness had descended upon me again. We held each other in tears for some time after.

Thanks to one of my partner's friends, I registered on the NHS App, which allows me access to all correspondence, records, and results relating to my health.

Whilst trawling through my medical history, which is really only the last few years, I found a report detailing what I had. It is a single large lesion, around five centimetres in size, that was located in segments 2 and 3 of my liver. I quickly looked at a diagram of a liver and was pleased to see that segments 2 and 3 are not in the main body of the liver; they make up a triangular section of the left-hand side of the liver (left lobe), which should mean that you are cutting off and not cutting into the main body of the liver.

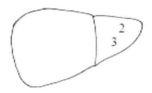

Diagram of the location of the lesion

There was also talk of cutting the gallbladder out at the same time, because if there was a problem later on with the gallbladder, it could be more difficult to deal with after a resection had taken place, or it might simply be obstructing surgery.

There are a lot of treatments available for people with my condition (secondary liver cancer), some of which relate to people who are unable to have surgery, which are aimed at managing and controlling the cancer by slowing down or shrinking the cancer and improving quality of life by relieving symptoms; treatments such as chemotherapy, hormonal therapy, targeted therapy, immunotherapy, tumour ablation, embolisation treatment, radiotherapy, as well as supportive or palliative treatments. The treatment you have will depend upon the primary cancer it has spread from, what part of the liver has been affected, and if any other parts of the body have been affected [35].

After spending time reading about the options available, I sent an email to the colorectal nurses full of questions. Not long after, I received a call from the lead nurse, who was able to put my mind at rest. I asked why a biopsy was not being done to see if it was benign before surgery took place. The answer made good sense: to take a sample, you will disturb the surface, as you ideally need to cut a piece out for analysis, which if cancerous could then lead to cancer cells escaping.

This made me think about the tumour in my colon and the fact that they took a number of samples from it, but then I remembered that there was already blood swirling around it, hence the microscopic traces of blood found in my stool sample, so cutting a piece out wasn't going to make a difference with regards to anything escaping. I think the horse had already bolted! I suppose it helped that they would be flushed out of my system when I went to the loo.

When we discussed the location of it and its size, another good point was made: that it was better to have one large, accessible tumour in an area that can be easily cut away than having numerous smaller tumours in the main body of the liver, which were difficult to access.

We discussed the pre-op, which was over a week away, and I reiterated what I had emailed to the other nurses: that I wanted it as soon as possible, as a date for surgery would not be given until I had been assessed; therefore, I would accept any time and date that was sooner, provided I was given a minimum of two hours' notice. I made it very clear that I wanted the procedure to be carried out as soon as possible.

Before the pre-op could take place, I had to supply another blood sample. These normally have to be booked at the hospital via their website, but there would have been a one-week delay; therefore, I popped to the phlebotomy department, which was next door, explained my situation to the nurse, and had a sample taken within half an hour. I went back to the nurses to let them know that it had been done, pointing at my watch for them to 'crack on.'

Chemotherapy was discussed, and I was told that would be down to oncology and would be dependent upon the results of the surgery. The use of immunotherapy was also discussed, and again, I was told that this would fall under oncology's wing.

As I did for my first operation, I enquired whether I could

have a private room, which I would be happy to pay for. I was told that such a question had never been asked before, but they would look into it for me.

After surgery, I would be on their radar for ten years, and after two years, scans would be annually and not six monthly. I was pleased with the conversation we had, as it put a lot of questions and worries to bed. I had also booked a meeting with a private consultant to ask them a host of questions about what was happening and what was proposed. I also had a video meeting with a consultant from The Cancer Screening Trust. It probably sounds over the top, but if it puts my mind at ease and I fully understand what is going on, then it will have been worth it.

I think that it is always worth getting different opinions and perspectives on something so important; after all, it is not like I am trying to decide what colour paint best suits the lounge; it is about my life and my existence. I think that is important enough to go the extra mile, even if I do pee people off with all my questions and urgency. What I cannot allow to happen is for me to be sat thinking, 'I wish I had done 'x, y, or z,' but it is too late now.'

The next day, I received a call from pre-op saying that they had received a call asking them to bring my date forward. I gladly took the date, which meant that my results would be discussed a week earlier than what had been previously arranged. The lead nurse commented that it was good that I was showing an interest in what was going on; it certainly was, as I would now be discussed at the MDT meeting a week earlier. With this fresh news in mind, I booked a hotel within walking distance of the hospital as it was an early appointment forty miles away, and I could not afford to be late.

In my mind, you have a couple of options: you can just leave it to the people that are dealing with you and accept what is given to you, or you can show an interest and try to get the best for yourself. I value my life and my relationship, and I want it to continue for as long as possible, so I will carry on showing an interest, I will continue to ask questions, and I will continue to be a pain in the arse if need be.

The next day, I had a meeting with a private consultant. We spoke openly for an hour, and they were able to answer questions that the nurses were not able to. They reiterated a lot of what I had already been told, which was good, but were able to answer other queries too, such as the option of going private.

On a positive note, after discussing my health and habits in general, the private consultant commented that they thought I would sail through the pre-op, but not to underestimate the size and importance of the operation that I was going to have. It was interesting to note that both the lead nurse and the consultant commented on how major an operation it was – much more so than my previous operation.

One of the questions that I wanted to ask them was about

going private. I had asked this when I had my first operation and had a feeling that I would be experiencing déjà vu, and I was right.

Because the operation is so specialised, there are limited hospitals that will be able to cater to my needs. If I were to change hospital and consultant, the process would have to start from scratch; however, the surgeon that is dealing with me does carry out private work; therefore, there would be continuity and little delay, albeit at a different hospital. I was advised that, due to the surgery being so specialised, it would not be cheap. It would most likely be in the early tens of thousands, and if I needed additional time in the ICU, then the cost could increase even further.

I had also thought about aftercare such as chemotherapy and asked, 'If I went private, the cost of treatments such as chemotherapy, etc. would be additional costs; therefore, how easy a transition is it to go back to the NHS after having private surgery?' The answer was that it would be easy; it would not be a problem, which was reassuring. I think if you are going to go private, you need to make your decision very early on. In fact, the sooner the better.

One thing that was on my mind was managing my own scans and blood tests in conjunction with what the NHS had planned. I could have these done privately at my local private hospital, at one of The Cancer Screening Trust's locations, or at many other locations throughout the UK. I would look to have blood tests every three to four months and a CT, PET, or MRI scan every six months. I would not be happy leaving it longer than six months, certainly not twelve months; therefore, I would be paying for one scan per year.

The thought process is that the longer you stay without cancer, the less likely it is to reoccur. I think I will stick with my 'belt and braces' approach.

Immunotherapy is also of interest to me. This is a form of treatment that helps the immune system locate and attack cancer cells through the use of drugs. There are many types of immunotherapies, some of which can have serious side-effects if not treated [36]. It will be something that I will be discussing with my oncologist should I need any further treatment. Hopefully I won't, as the thought of having to go through chemotherapy again worries me greatly, as I only just managed to get through the first lot of treatment. It was horrendous.

Whilst sat typing, I received a phone call confirming that if the date was acceptable to me, I had been provisionally booked in to have my operation just three days after my pre-op. I also received a call from the private consultant saying that they had looked at my scan and, bearing in mind my recent news, I should stick with the plan and proceed with the NHS. This makes it just over five weeks from my initial call to the colorectal nurses chasing my blood results to having the operation. I cannot tell you how grateful I am to those involved.

The pre-op meeting went well. I had an ECG, an MRSA swab, a blood sample was taken, my pulse was taken, my blood pressure was taken, my height and weight were recorded, and I met with an anaesthetist who talked me through the procedure and the risks involved. He was very nice, made me feel at ease, and was very easy to talk to.

Unlike the first operation's pre-op assessment, this anaesthetist actually discussed post-op pain relief in detail rather than just going on about my likelihood of dying on the operating table! I had read the pamphlets and had opted for PCA (patient-controlled analgesia) for after the operation and a local anaesthetic wound infusion for during the operation.

PCA is what I requested for my first operation but never received. It is a way for the patient to administer pain relief themselves after the operation by simply pressing a button on a hand-held device. An anaesthetic wound infusion consists of inserting a very fine tube around the wound area, which delivers preset amounts of anaesthetic to the patient via a pump.

We also touched on the probability of me not surviving the operation, which was one in fifty! This meant that I was six times more likely to die than when I had my first operation. One in fifty sounds really bad, but when you translate it into a percentage, it works out at just 2%. One in fifty sounds much worse than 2%.

The risk of death was actually quoted as being between 3% and 5% in the letter that I received following my meeting with the consultant, along with other risks such as bleeding, injury to other structures, a 5% risk of bile leak, a 5% risk of wound infection, and a risk of chronic pain and medical complications. At the end of the day, you make your choice between the risk of having major surgery with the aim of removing the cancer completely or you choose managing the cancer on an ongoing basis. I wanted it out, and as soon as possible!

The positive thing from my perspective was that my blood pressure was never mentioned, as I am now taking blood pressure tablets and it is under control.

It is a long way from the five months that I had to wait for my first operation from being diagnosed to having the operation, but I have COVID to thank for that! Maybe next time people will take heed of the warnings that they are given in relation to life-threatening viruses, because there will be more of them if we do not stop treating wildlife the way that we do. If I'd had the first operation sooner, then I probably wouldn't have needed this operation, as it wouldn't have had time to spread.

Now that I had a date for the operation, I booked a hotel for the night before for my partner and I, as I had to be there for seven o'clock in the morning, so even staying at a hotel within walking distance still made it an early start, especially as I had to have a shower before I had surgery using a special antibacterial body wash that had been given to me.

My partner is not a confident driver and hadn't driven far before; therefore, she drove us to the hospital the Sunday before the operation so that she knew where she was going on the day and where the car parks were when she came to visit. This was different too, as being in a COVID-free hospital before visitors were not allowed.

Throughout the five weeks, besides being involved in all of the medical meetings and tests, I had been busy reviewing our finances and creating spreadsheets for my partner detailing all of the pensions, savings, and various scenarios should she want to stop working. This was extremely hard, as I was putting things in place should I not make it.

We reviewed our wills, renewed them, and applied for power of attorney (health and financial) for each other, as we never got around to doing it when I had my first operation. The seriousness of the operation really hit home to both of us, so we decided that we would have a simple wedding at a registry office as a mark of our love and commitment to each other, as well as inheritance tax implications should I not make it! I wanted to do everything I could to make my partner's life as easy as possible, should the worst happen.

While all of this was going on, a friend messaged me, asking how I felt. I said, 'nervous, scared, but I knew that I had to have the operation if I wanted the best outcome and to spend more time with my partner.' It is sod's law again that I find myself cancelling another hotel booking and giving away tickets, as we were due to be away at an international horse trial, which was a week after my proposed date for surgery; however, it is a small price to pay for being dealt with so quickly.

I am so grateful to those who made it possible, and so quickly too. Things happened so fast that I never received correspondence; I just received phone calls, as letters would take too long to get through the system. In fact, I got a copy of my letter relating to when I was going to have my operation around two months later! Thank you so much to all involved for pushing me through the system so quickly and for giving me another chance.

9

Operation 2 – liver resection

On numerous occasions, I have been told of the magnitude of this operation compared to my first operation. The liver is a vital organ, just as the heart is. The liver is responsible for storing blood (it holds around 13% of the body's blood at any given time) as well as performing in excess of five hundred functions [37]. It is also the only organ that can regenerate. It is said that it can regrow within four to six weeks, depending upon each individual's health and circumstances. For some, it may take longer.

When I was in the meeting with the consultant, one of the forms that I had to sign apart from the consent form was a blood transfusion form, which makes sense bearing in mind some of the liver's functions. In fact, it was marked as a 'probable' requirement on the consent form. The official name of my operation is a left hepatectomy with a +/- cholecystectomy, which relates to the removal of segments two and three of the liver; however, if the lesion is close enough to segment four, a part of this may also be removed. The +/- cholecystectomy relates to whether the gallbladder is removed or not.

The morning of the operation, I showered using the antibacterial wash given to me and had drank the 'booster' drinks given to me at the pre-op. My partner drove me to the hospital, and we sat in the arrivals ward waiting. Within a short period of time, I was booked in and sent to a room where I could get changed into a gown.

The anaesthetist who was looking after me came along and introduced himself, and we discussed pain relief. The refreshing thing was that he said that it was my call and that I could have what I wanted. We agreed on what I had chosen, and that was it. Job done!

Not long after, I said goodbye to my partner and was wheeled off to see the anaesthetist. As we sped down the corridor, I shouted 'look out' to my partner as we nearly ran her over due to her stepping out of a passageway right in front of us!

The nurse and I waited outside. We were both freezing cold. I was visibly shaking; it was that bad. I cannot remember anything from then on, apart from waking up in a ward and hearing people shouting and swearing. I later found out that this was the 'recovery' area where people were dropped off after surgery waiting to be taken to whatever ward they needed to go to. It was horrific. I was in that awful place for around three hours, drifting in and out of consciousness.

The operation took around three and a half hours as it was open surgery. Once finished, the surgeon called my partner in person, which was very thoughtful of him, to let her know that everything had gone according to plan and that I would be transferred to the ICU for observation.

I don't really remember much of the rest of the first day. The second day, I was helped out of bed and sat in a chair. It was a real struggle, as I had so many tubes and cables connected to me that it was impossible to move. There was no way that I was going to be able to walk anywhere. This was to prove the worst thing about my stay – my restricted movement thanks to all the tubes, etc.

I had a clip on my finger attached to a cord, a cannula in my wrist, a cannula (main line) in my neck, a catheter up my wiener, a drain tube in my abdomen attached to a bag, anaesthetic tubes, as well as the compression wraps on my calves attached to me. I couldn't even turn over in bed.

After spending twenty minutes sitting in a chair by my bed, I asked to get back into bed as I was getting cold. I couldn't walk anywhere, so there was nothing that I could do. I called my partner to let her know how I was and that it wasn't worth visiting me that day as I wasn't up to it, and to come the next day instead.

During the morning, I had a visit and was told how well the operation had gone, that there was minimal blood loss, that another scan had been carried out after the operation, and that they couldn't see anything to worry about. During the operation, the surgeon has a good look around to check for any abnormalities or further spreading of the cancer. Thankfully, none were seen.

They were very interested in how I got on with my pain relief options and asked what my level of pain was from one to ten;

I said about two. I wasn't actually in pain; I was just tender and sore around the wound area. I stopped taking oral painkillers for this reason, as I did after my first operation.

Besides the soreness and frustration of being wrapped up in tubes and cables, I felt very queasy, tired, bloated, and constipated. I laid there trying to get comfortable by adjusting the bed's position, as I was now getting backache from lying down for so long. I just wanted to get up and walk freely.

That night I was asked if I was using my PCA, and I said that I was not, as I wasn't in any pain. Don't get me wrong, I was sore and tender and a bit light-headed and queasy, but I wasn't requiring pain relief. I was told that I should use it, as it would help me sleep. I thought this to be a good idea, as I'd had little sleep for a couple of days. Little did I know what a mistake this turned out to be!

The drug used for my PCA was fentanyl. To try and get some sleep, I started pressing the button to administer the drug. This turned out to be one of the worst nights of my life, as my level of anxiety went through the roof and was verging on paranoia. Every time a nurse came to see me, I was asking them what they were doing and why they were doing it. If I heard the slightest noise, I was looking to see what it was. I honestly thought that the nurses were out to finish me off.

At the same time, my heart rate went off the chart. I remember laying there thinking that one way or another, I was going to die that night; either the nurses would kill me or I would have a heart attack! So much for a good night's sleep! Needless to say, I never used it again.

Day three started with one of the consultant's morning visits. We talked about how I was feeling, and I was again asked if I was in much pain. I commented that I was not really in any pain and that the tubes attached to me were driving me mad, as they were preventing me from moving. They commented that they had heard that I was on my feet and able to walk the day after my operation, saying that it was remarkable that I could do this after such a major operation but that it was not recommended! I think that was a polite way of telling me off.

Shortly after, a couple of nurses came around and spoke to me about moving me to a normal ward, as I had been hinting that I would prefer to stay where I was due to it being quiet. They explained that coming from the ICU onto a normal ward was the precursor to leaving, and that if I stayed on an ICU ward, it would most likely prolong my stay. They also tempted me with an air bed, which would be much more comfortable than the one I was in, as well as the fact that they would prep me for leaving by taking the attachments off me. This did it for me; I was transferred to a ward of six later that day.

I had been lucky enough to have been looked after by a male nurse, who was a gentle giant. He was considerate, kind, and thoughtful, and he understood my frustration at not being able to move. He gave me a couple of body washes, for which

I was grateful, and arranged for the catheter and the leg pressure wraps to be removed. This was much appreciated, but it still left me no closer to being able to move freely.

My partner was there when they were removed. The removal of the catheter was funny, as it was completely opposite to how it had been removed during my first operation.

The nurse, during the first operation, withdrew it nice and slowly, whereas this nurse told me that she was going to pull it out quickly and that I was to relax beforehand, which is easier said than done, especially when you have an audience! She counted down, and then, with one pull, it was out.

In the early hours of the morning, I needed to pee. Thankfully, I had already asked for some cardboard urinals to be at hand should I need to go. My problem was that I had to shuffle to the end of the bed, manoeuvre my way between the bed rails, stand up without pulling any of the tubes out, get the urinal, and then pee.

As my bladder had become used to just peeing when it wanted to via the catheter, I didn't have a great deal of time to get myself sorted. I managed to stand up, and as I was trying to pull the curtains around for some privacy, my bladder let go. Thankfully, it was just a spurt to start with and not the whole lot. I managed to complete my pee in the urinal when a nurse walked up and asked what was going on. I told them that I'd had my catheter removed and that I'd had an accident.

I suppose one thing that was different from before was that I had brought around twelve small bottles of water with me, so my fluid intake was much greater. I hardly drank any water during my first operation, just a couple of small bottles of fizzy drinks.

Rather than helping me, they just stood there watching, offering no assistance while I cleaned the floor, changed my socks and underwear, and then made the bed! I couldn't believe it. As the compression socks were now wet, I put my own socks on. I asked if they wanted me to put some more compression socks on in relation to DVT. They said that they would sort it out in the morning.

This was only my second day after my operation, and I was being allowed to stand, walk, bend, and lift without any help. I was pretty angry at the lack of assistance offered and the fact that they did not seem bothered about DVT either. I wonder what the consultant, who commented on me walking so early, would have said if he had found out. I think he would have done his nut!

If I cast my mind back to when I had my first operation, I would get told off for crossing my legs as it can reduce blood flow, and I was told that I would need to wear the compression socks for three weeks. They were very strict. It seemed like the opposite here. The fact that the first hospital wanted me up and about as soon as possible was also different. At this hospital there was little to no encouragement to get me mobile; I had to fight for it.

Day four started with me asking about compression socks. Needless to say, nothing happened. The morning progressed as usual with an entourage of nurses and a consultant. I explained to them that I was desperate to be disconnected completely so that I could walk around and get some sleep. They agreed and confirmed that I would be disconnected. I also said that I would recover better whilst at home, as I would eat and sleep properly, to which they also agreed.

To throw a curved ball, I started getting pains in my chest. They started in the middle of my chest and emanated outward. I mentioned it to a nurse, and a doctor came to give me an ECG. I had two in total and was given the all clear. I wondered whether it had anything to do with the fentanyl. On top of the acute anxiety caused by the fentanyl and the stress I was incurring due to not being able to move and not eating or sleeping properly for days, maybe my body was trying to tell me something? It'd had enough!

My partner came to visit again, and I told her the good news. It was a busy day, as it was a bank holiday and there were lots of visitors, so we pulled the curtain around for some privacy. Not long after, a nurse appeared to change my dressings. She also gave me a load of spare ones for the nurse at my GP surgery to use once I was discharged.

I was now feeling really quite rough, as I had not eaten properly for four days, apart from some soup and ice cream, and I hadn't slept properly for four days either. I was desperate to get home now.

The problem was that I found the quality of the food to be poor, and I was still feeling queasy. This was not helped when I had a tuna sandwich, which tasted bitter and made me feel sick for a couple of days. It was rank. Cereal was poured into an odd-shaped bowl, which created two layers. The bottom layer of cereal was sat in 'warm' milk, and the top layer had no milk. By the time I had eaten the top layer, the bottom layer was soggy and inedible.

Later that day, my prayers were answered when I was completely disconnected. It was a joyous occasion. We celebrated this by finding some stairs and a long corridor to walk up and down. As before, I had no problem with climbing up and down four flights of stairs or walking a reasonable distance. After this, my partner made her way home. I relished my new-found freedom by getting my own clothes and toiletries out of my bag and making my way to the washroom.

Just before I left the ward, a physio came to see me and asked how I was getting on. I explained that I had just been disconnected, that I had walked up and down stairs as well as down a long corridor, and that I felt fine. I also explained that I had been doing deep breathing exercises to ensure that the bottom of my lungs didn't collapse due to being laid down for so long. They were more than happy with this and confirmed that they would sign me off as fit to go. Another box ticked!

This time, I was pleased that I had packed everything I had, as I was using most of it. I laid my clothes out that I was going to get changed into and got my toiletries ready. I then stripped; this was the first time that I had properly seen my wound. I was mortified at what I saw. It was much bigger than I expected.

The wound was around 300mm long (approx. 12 inches). To put it into perspective, that is over one sixth of my height! To make matters worse, it was covered in a black film about a centimetre wide. I later found out that this was glue. I looked, but I could not see any signs of stitches or staples. Later on, it was confirmed that I had been glued together! Incredible.

After the shock of seeing my wounds, I had a full body wash, brushed my teeth, and got changed into my own clean clothes. It was such a pleasure to be able to walk around free of tubes.

When I got back to the ward, I asked a nurse if they could change my bed for me, as I had just had a body wash, had put my own clean clothes on, and did not want to get into a bed full of blood-stained sheets. It was agreed to, although I felt begrudgingly, and I climbed into a nice fresh bed. Bliss!

Rather than using headphones, I put my phone on my pillow next to my ear, turned the volume right down, and listened to various stories and music that I had loaded onto my phone all the way through the night until morning. I could now relax for the first time in four days.

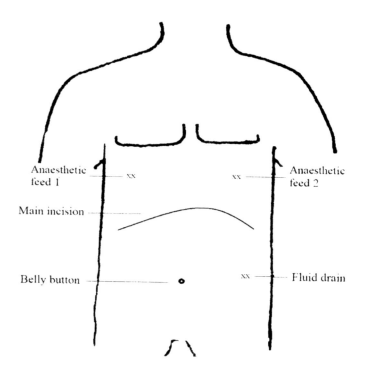

Diagram of the incisions and insertions

Day five began as usual with a walkabout of nurses and a consultant. As they approached me, the consultant shouted my name and asked how I was as he thrust his hand into mine. I told him that I had climbed stairs, had been for a long walk, and that I had given myself a full body wash, put clean clothes on, had my bed changed, and that I was feeling good.

After answering a few more questions, he asked me if I wanted to go home, to which I replied, 'I would, very much so.' He then shouted, 'Get this man home today.' All the consultants came across as consummate professionals, something that I respect. They weren't aloof or standoffish at all, which made conversation easier. After they had left, I quickly messaged my partner with the good news, saying that I would let her know when I would be ready to collect. I had matched the time that I stayed in hospital for my first operation – that was also five days!

Shortly after the consultant had left, I was offered some toast and marmalade. I had it during my first stay in hospital, and it was great; however, this toast had been produced en masse and had been covered by tin foil. This meant that the condensation from the hot toast formed on the inside of the tin foil and then dropped down on the toast, creating warm, soggy, limp toast! I did actually lose my temper, as I was so looking forward to it. I swore and threw it back on the plate, cursing. How can you get something so simple so wrong?

That was it; no more meals from this hospital. I messaged my partner with a list of meals and foods that I would like for when I was at home. She was taking the rest of the week off to look after me to make sure that I behaved myself and didn't overdo it.

My time from then on was spent talking to a guy on the ward who recognised the baseball cap that I was wearing, as it was associated with horse riding. He had a horse, and so we talked for quite a while. It turned out that his operation had been cancelled due to one of his lungs collapsing at the bottom. During my previous stay in hospital, the physio brought a piece of apparatus around which you blew into to exercise your lungs. They also requested that I do deep breathing exercises to maintain my lung capacity and health. None of this had been discussed during this stay.

Later on, another physio came around and saw me up and about talking to people and commented that there was no point in asking whether I was mobile or not. They came just to check on what had been said to the other physio, and after a few minutes, they went away happy wishing me well.

I asked various nurses on the ward when I was going to be discharged so that I could let my partner know, as it was an hour's drive. I never did get an answer. Instead, after lunch, a guy arrived pushing a wheelchair and calling my name out. I told him who I was, to which he replied that he had come to take me to the discharge ward. I told him that he would have to give me five minutes, as I had not packed because no one had told me when I was going.

I quickly threw everything into my bags, shook the guy's hand, who I had been talking to earlier, and sat in the wheelchair. It was a long journey across the sprawling hospital, which was taken at breakneck speed. We arrived at the discharge ward, and he shot off to transport someone else wherever they needed to go.

The discharge area was a small, seated area where people waited for their medication and release. It was very busy, with both patients and nurses coughing and sneezing. It really was not a place that I wanted to be. Needless to say, I was wearing a mask, as the last thing I wanted was a bad cough or to catch a bug with the wound that I had. It would have been a nightmare.

I messaged my partner that I would meet them at the entrance. After what seemed forever, I received my medication and asked if someone could help me with my bags, as it was a long walk to the entrance. After twenty minutes or so, my partner arrived, and we embraced, shed more tears, and went home.

My time in this hospital was very different from the first, in that COVID-19 was now no longer a threat; therefore, there was intermingling of patients and visitors, which meant that it was more crowded and there was nowhere that I could go to get away from people for some peace and quiet; I had people-free corridors and stairs, as well as a bay and snug room to myself before.

Then again, because of COVID, it took around five months to have my operation instead of five to six weeks! Even though I prefer peace and quiet and my own company, I would have preferred the much shorter lead time. I then probably would not have needed a second operation, as it would have stayed at stage 2 and would not have spread.

10

Recuperation

This recovery was completely different from my first operation, as that was largely based around diet, whereas this is more based around building energy levels back up and healing.

For me, recovery from my operation is orientated around maintaining energy levels, rest and relaxation, and exercise. I was told that I would see my energy levels plummet after surgery and that it would be a very slow recovery to get back to normal. It could be months.

When I was discharged after my first operation, I was given lots of high-calorie drinks to take home. This time, I received none, which did not make any sense to me, as I was continually told that it was a much bigger operation than before and that my energy levels would crash a week or so after the operation. Surely, it would have made sense to provide me with energy drinks to help sustain my recovery?

I think my stamina and the way that I work at home have allowed my body to cope with surgery, lack of food, etc. When I am at home, I can spend six or seven hours gardening, washing windows, cleaning gutters, washing cars, and so on. While I am outside, I will, more often than not, not have anything to eat or drink and will take the shortest of breaks. If my body is used to this kind of abuse, then it will help it cope with surgery and a lack of food and water. I think it has certainly helped my body cope in relation to what it has had to endure.

The first week at home, I was looked after by my partner and given strict instructions not to do anything. I did as I was told and rested completely for the first week. I sat in a recliner with a DVD on and nodded off when I needed to. Bearing in mind my lack of sleep and food, my energy levels were at zero anyway. I needed a week to recover before thinking about doing anything else.

Getting in and out of bed or even a chair proved difficult to start with, as I would normally use my stomach muscles. I found that leaning forward and putting my arm behind me allowed me to push myself upright in a chair so that I could then stand up by using my hands to push on the armrests.

To get into bed, I found that sitting on the edge of the bed and naturally allowing my body to lower itself sideways onto the mattress helped, as again, I barely needed to use my stomach muscles.

I found one of the worst things to do was to pull myself up the bed using my stomach muscles. One night, I did it out of habit and felt a searing pain; it felt like I had torn something deep inside my abdomen. From then on, if I needed to move up or down the bed, I would reverse my getting-in procedure. I would lay on my side and push myself up to the sitting position whilst lowering my legs to the floor. I would then sit further up or down the bed and then use my getting-in procedure again. It sounds long-winded, but it saves pulling something. In the early days, I found it very useful. I really didn't want to end up in A&E because I had injured myself doing something so basic.

If I needed to pick something up, rather than bend down and use my stomach muscles, I would use my knees to lower myself. You find different ways of doing things to prevent hurting yourself. After all, who wants to be back in a hospital due to damaging their wound or having a hernia to contend with?

I found walking to be excellent exercise. It not only kept me upright rather than stooping, but it also got me out of the house and breathing some fresh air.

Around a week after I was discharged, I went to see the nurse at my GP surgery to have my dressings changed. I prebooked slots every few days to have them changed over a ten-day period. After that, my wounds had sufficiently healed. The main wound had never had a dressing on it apart from the glue covering it; it was just a case of keeping it clean and dry.

During my hospitalisation, I had been told that I must keep the wound dry at all times. If I did get it wet, then I was to pat it dry with a clean towel rather than wiping it. I suppose the glue had bonded to the scab, so if I wiped the glue, I might pull the scab off too, which could lead to bleeding or worse.

While I was with the nurse, I mentioned that my left calf had lost a lot of muscle mass and that both calves were tender to touch. There was no bruising, swelling, or redness, but they (especially the left one) felt quite different. She immediately picked up on the threat of DVT and requested a doctor have a look. While we were waiting, she did a finger prick blood test to see if I was more or less likely to develop DVT. If it tested positive, it did not mean that I would develop DVT; it meant that I was more likely to develop it than not. It came back positive – I was more likely to develop it!

This makes sense, and this is why I worried about the lack of discipline I encountered relating to DVT at the hospital, because I know that I heal fast, and that means that I clot quickly.

As a precaution, I was given a higher dose of anticoagulants to take and was booked in for an ultrasound scan at my local hospital a few days later. I attended my appointment, and ten minutes later I was given the all clear, along with a comment that I had beautiful veins! There's a first!

Unfortunately, I had to take anticoagulant injections for three weeks after I returned home. I would not have minded if they were like the previous syringes that pushed into your skin like a hot knife through butter. These syringes were awful. The needle was difficult to push into the skin, and when I pulled it out, my skin stuck to the needle. No matter how hard I pushed on the plunger, the sheath would not come out to cover the needle. I needed two hands to push it to get the sheath release to work once it had been extracted.

Sometimes, it bled where I had injected, which it never did before, and it caused yellow bruising around the area where I had been injecting. After three weeks of injecting myself, the area where I had injected was still bruised, sore, and tender, and two months later, it is still tender. I got to dread injecting myself in the evening. I felt more pain doing that than I did after my operation!

As well as the injections, I was given some morphine for pain relief, which I have never used, along with stool softeners and laxatives, as the amount and type of drugs that I had been given can cause constipation. I did take these for a couple of weeks to help me get back to normal.

One really strange after-effect of the operation or the drugs that I had been given was that when I was in bed and I turned from lying on my side (either side) to lying flat on my back, my stomach muscles contracted really tightly, followed by my thigh and calf muscles. This contraction lasted around five seconds, and then I returned to normal. I could not stop it; it just happened automatically.

With regards to walking, I took my first steps outside of the house during the first week, just to get out of the house and get some fresh air. One thing that I found was that whatever top I wore, even a lightweight t-shirt, rubbed against my wound, making it sore. To overcome this, I ended up walking around the house with my t-shirt rolled up and pegged above my wound. While I was walking outside, I would put my fists under my t-shirt to create a gap, thus preventing rubbing. It may sound daft, but it meant that I was more comfortable and could walk further and easier.

A week after being home, I completed my first half-mile walk. Five days later, I completed two half-mile walks in a day. I kept walking each day until I achieved a continuous three-mile walk at a normal pace just over three weeks after coming home. Around the same time, I called my insurer about driving. They were not helpful at all, saying that it was down to my GP or surgeon. I gave up in the end and told them that I had performed two emergency stops and that I could do it without a problem. I was ready to go!

Like before, it was great to be behind the wheel again. I just did local trips to the shops to start with. I went shopping around the same time, pushing a trolley rather than carrying bags around, and just got the essentials. Every little step was a step closer to normality.

Do you know what caused me the most discomfort whilst driving? It wasn't the seatbelt pressing against my wound or getting in and out of the car; it was in fact the appalling condition of our roads. The unevenness, lumps, bumps, and potholes gave me the most discomfort! How bad is that?

Around four weeks after the operation, I received a phone call asking me if I could meet the consultant the next day. I had been waiting for a letter, as I knew it was time for a meeting. I was keen to meet him so that I could ask him numerous questions, the most important being: if he was happy with how it went, if I needed chemotherapy, and if I should be looking out for any signs.

My partner and I rolled up early and saw him within a few minutes of arriving. It was a very different meeting than before; it was more relaxed and communicative. He said that it was an unremarkable operation in that it went to plan with no issues and that I did not need chemotherapy. I was so pleased to hear that.

We were told that segments 2 and 3 and a portion of segment 4 of my liver had been removed, which equated to around 25% of my liver. My gallbladder remained intact, and I had no gallstones.

I told him about my progress and then started reeling off my questions when he started laughing. I don't think anyone had asked him so many questions, some of which he couldn't answer. I was conscious of taking his time up and so asked my final question, 'Are there any symptoms that I should be looking out for with regards to reoccurrence?' I don't think he had met anyone like me before.

His answer was interesting. He told me to not think about it and to get on with my life and enjoy myself. His other comment was that if I did not stop thinking about it, it would destroy me mentally. I fully concur with this, which was one of the main reasons why I did not include the life expectancies of certain cancers in this book.

The meeting ended with us discussing blood tests and CT scans. They were going to book a CT scan when I told them that I already had one booked for three months' time. This is where the confusion started, as I am still being monitored by the original team for another two years, and now I am being monitored by the new team for ten years, so there is an overlap. The original team is now extending their time between tests, whereas the new team will be testing more frequently. It did not help when I received blood test forms through the post with no date on them.

The consultant was happy with the date of the CT scan that had already been arranged, but there was confusion over when the blood test was required because I already had one booked pre-CT scan and a CEA test for ten weeks' time.

I had the blood test taken a month after seeing the consultant, and I am pleased to say that my markers had dropped to 2.2, which was great news. My markers seemed to be working this time! One thing that I am waiting for are the results from what was taken out of me – was it definitely cancer, and if so, how bad was it?

After visiting the NHS App weeks later, I found a letter relating to my operation, the histology, and the staging of what was taken out of me. Histology relates to the study of cells and tissue under a microscope.

The operation was a left partial hepatectomy with segments 2, 3, and a part of segment 4 of my liver being resected. There was an 8mm margin around the cut, which was said to be clear. The tumour was a metastatic adenocarcinoma, which was moderately differentiated and was described by histological staging as G2 V0 R0. Let me explain:

The grade relates to how differentiated cells are, e.g.,
X – not assessable.
1 – well differentiated.
2 – moderately differentiated.
3 – poorly differentiated.
4 – undifferentiated [38].

The lower the number, the more normal the cancer cells look, and the higher the number, the more abnormal the cancer cells look. The numbers also relate to how fast the cancer cells are likely to grow and spread, with 4 being the most aggressive and 1 being the least aggressive [39]. Mine was G2 – moderately differentiated, so not too aggressive.

V relates to vascular spread, which is the invasion of nearby blood vessels. Thankfully, mine was 0, so there was no vascular invasion.

R relates to whether any residual tumour has been left after resection, e.g.,
X – not assessable.
0 – no residual tumour.
1 – microscopic residual tumour.
2 – macroscopic residual tumour [40].

If something is microscopic, it can only be seen by using a microscope, whereas something that is macroscopic can be seen without the need for a microscope.

Not long after I had received my results, I spoke to the private consultant with whom I had been dealing, who confirmed that the R0 result was very significant in that it raised my predicted life expectancy by more than 50%.

I was extremely pleased with the positive results, especially the R0 result; however, I spent a week trying to understand if a mistake had been made, as there was mention of both V0 and V2, which could have quite a different outcome in relation to my prognosis. I am pleased to say that it is V0.

Whilst speaking to the consultant about my results, he also mentioned that if reoccurrence were to take place, it would be sooner rather than later. I suppose this relates back to the frequency of checks diminishing as more time passes.

I am now seven weeks after surgery and am doing the shopping as normal, driving further, and have been out cutting bushes in the garden. Don't get me wrong; when I feel I have had enough, I will stop, come in, and put a DVD on. The last thing I want to do is take a step back. There is no hard-and-fast rule as to what and how much you should do, just recommendations and a dash of common sense. It is up to each individual to be sensible and to gauge their limits.

With regards to my wound, it is now completely clear of glue and scabs, which meant that I could have my first shower in over six weeks; it was so good. My tummy is still sore and a bit swollen, and my wound's swelling has reduced considerably. I take ibuprofen twice a day, as it helps reduce inflammation and swelling.

I admitted to my partner a week ago that I had overdone it and that I would be taking a step back to sit and update this book, which I am doing. I am enjoying engaging my brain again and thinking rather than doing.

Where do I go from here? I will complete my book and get it registered with the relevant libraries. I have been in contact with various colorectal departments in hospitals throughout the UK and have sent copies of my original 'test' book to see what response I get.

The one thing that still remains is a feeling of fatigue, both mentally and physically. I have heard the mental tiredness referred to as 'brain fog.' It is like my brain is numb; I don't feel as sharp as I should, and my memory is lacking. Hopefully this will clear and I will get back to normal.

I also suffer from bouts of depression, and I feel a rage in me for no particular reason. Physically, I recovered very quickly, but mentally, I think I am still catching up with the realisation of what happened to me and what I went through.

Am I free from cancer? I have no idea. Of course, I hope I am, but I cannot say for certain. It looks like there has been no spread from the new tumour, but that doesn't mean to say that there aren't cells still circulating from the original tumour. As time ticks by (it has been nearly three years since my first diagnosis), I would like to think that the chances of me developing it again are getting less.

I hope that I am clear, as I am not sure that I could cope with more invasive tests and operations. Throughout my journey, I talk about wanting to be there for my partner and not wanting to leave her on her own, and this has not changed. After a while though, all the prodding and poking has started to take its toll mentally. I just want to be left alone and not have to worry about the results of the next blood test or scan. I have had enough. There comes a point when you just want to be left alone. Perhaps that is why I have this anger inside of me.

I am not saying that I am giving up; I suppose what I am trying to convey is that the more it goes on, the more difficult it becomes to 'fight the fight.' For me, it is a mental fight more than a physical one. Like chemotherapy, it has become a war of attrition.

I remember my partner's father refusing chemotherapy and deciding to go on holiday with his wife rather than having to endure more treatment. I also remember a guy who attended the same chemotherapy clinic that I did, saying to the nurse that he had sold his house, had bought a camper van, and was going travelling with his dog. There comes a time when all you want to do is be left alone to enjoy the time that you have left. I can understand that completely.

I think that once you have been touched by this awful disease, you are very lucky not to get it again. Very lucky. For many people, unfortunately, it becomes a part of their and their family's lives.

What I do know is that I will do everything in my power to make a full recovery and carry on enjoying my life whilst still being involved in the monitoring process.

11

Cancer in general

Cancer has become the bane of modern life. In the UK, it has been said that one in two people will develop cancer during their lifetime. That is half of the population! Personally, I know of a friend's daughter who had it; two members of my partner's immediate family have had it, with one passing away; two friends fathers have passed away with it; a school friend has passed away due to it; four people that I know of near where I live have had it; two people I know have had skin cancer; friends and family of friends of my partner have had it and still have it; and a friend has had a polyp removed and underwent radiotherapy. You can't seem to get away from it, and the rate at which it is growing is frightening

It has been forecast that there will be an increase from 384,000 people developing cancer a year in the UK (2017-19) to 506,000 people in 2038-40 if current trends continue [41].

This could equate to 8.4 million new cases and 3.5 million people dying from it in the UK between 2023 and 2040 [42].

Globally, by 2040, there will be 28 million new cases of cancer each year. This is up from an estimated 18.1 million in 2020. Out of interest, the UK's incident rate is ranked higher than 90% of the world and higher than 75% of Europe [43]!

The question is, 'How is the NHS going to cope with an increase of nearly 31.8% in this timeframe? It is not as though oncologists (of which there are different types), oncology nurses, pathologists, anaesthetists, surgeons, consultants, radiologists, and countless others in the support chain grow on trees; they all need extensive training. This worries me greatly, as much as it worries me why we are seeing such a dramatic increase in cancer cases and why this god-awful disease is becoming a part of everyone's lives. We will look at causes of cancer in the next chapter.

So, what is cancer? How does it start, and how has it become so prevalent?

There are over two hundred forms of cancer. Over two hundred! Each of them has to be diagnosed and treated in a certain way [44]. This brings me back to the number of people who are going to have to be employed to cope with the forecast increase.

These are some of the two hundred cancers: breast, anal, penile, womb, cervical, brain tumour, eye, mouth, kidney, liver, lung, skin, bone, pancreatic, testicular, thyroid, bladder, and prostate, to name but a few. The four most common types of cancer in the UK are breast, lung, prostate, and bowel [45].

So, where does cancer come from, and how do we get it? Are we born with cancer cells in our bodies? Well, we don't have cancer cells in our body per se, but cells can mutate or become damaged and then form cancer cells, and damaged or changed cells can be inherited.

Cancer is caused by cells growing and reproducing uncontrollably. These cancerous cells can then damage and invade surrounding organs and tissue and spread to other parts of the body [46].

Cancer is a gene-based disease; normally cells die and are naturally replaced, but sometimes this replication goes wrong, which can be down to a number of factors: problems when cell division takes place, when genes that control cell division, growth, and function are changed, DNA being damaged due to chemicals (tobacco smoke, for example), as well as inheriting damaged or changed cells from parents. Cancer cells are different from normal cells in that they can continue growing even though the body has not told them to; they ignore the body telling them to die or to stop dividing; they can travel to and invade other areas of the body; and they can even con immune cells into protecting the tumour rather than attacking it! I find one of the most damning attributes of a tumour is that it can tell blood vessels to grow towards it, which then supply it with oxygen and nutrients; they even take its waste away [47]. Even some viruses can lead to cancer [48]! How can these cells become so clever and do so much? It is beyond me.

I used to liken cancer to a parasite, but of course it isn't, as a parasite is a foreign entity that enters a body and lives in or on it - malaria being an example. Cancer is primarily due to our body's cells changing and multiplying. However, having said that, certain viruses, infections, and chemicals that enter our body can trigger cancer, as can the way we live and eat. I suppose that is what I struggle with the most. Cancer can be a silent killer, caused by something that your body has absorbed or by your body itself. I felt as though my own body had failed me.

There is nothing simple or obvious about this disease, which is part of what makes it so deadly. The symptoms of cancer can also be confused with those of non-cancer-related illnesses. Let us have a look at a few:

- persistent coughing and hoarseness: I had both of these and was diagnosed with a pulled muscle in my throat. My mother had issues with acid reflux, which caused her similar symptoms. I also remember what was called the 'three-month cough' that was circulating some years ago.
- Heartburn and indigestion: these can be caused by diet, acid reflux, and stress.
- Feeling bloated and tired: these can be caused by the menopause as well as a lack of exercise and a poor diet.
- Passing blood in the urine: I know of two people who have had this happen, and neither were diagnosed with cancer. It can also be caused by a UTI or an enlarged prostate.
- Persistent bad headaches: this can be linked to menopause, muscle tension, eye strain, and stress.

- Blood from the bottom and in stools: this can be due to haemorrhoids and other rectal issues such as polyps.
- Tinnitus: I have it, and so does my partner. Infection, physical damage to the inner ear, or a problem between the brain and the ear when interpreting sound are among the numerous reasons why people have tinnitus.

I think the key word that relates to a lot of the symptoms is 'persistent,' i.e., if the symptoms carry on for a length of time.

Don't get me wrong; I am not trying to belittle or undermine the symptoms; what I am saying is that it is not that straightforward. Can you imagine if everyone with the above symptoms and changes to warts or moles went to see their GP? They would be inundated. The NHS is desperately trying to find cancer in its early stages by making people aware, but with the state of the NHS at the moment, it is a big ask.

The NHS waiting list for people waiting for consultant-led elective care in 2024 exceeded seven million [49] - that is more than ten percent of the UK population! It is not just the number of people on the waiting list that is worrying, but the time they are waiting too.

So, why are we getting more cancer diagnoses? Things like smoking, drinking, and obesity are reasons, but it is not just how we are getting it but the fact that we have an ageing population thanks to our excellent healthcare. Our ageing population certainly has something to do with the figures increasing, as over 65% of people in England in 2017 who were diagnosed with cancer were over 65 years old, and that figure is increasing. In the UK in 2017, one in every five people were aged 65 and over; this could reach one in every four people by 2037. That could be an increase from 18.2% to 24% [50]!

Why do the numbers of cases increase with age? Well, before damaged cells have the ability to turn cancerous, our body usually eliminates them, but the ability to do this decreases the older we become [51].

Let us have a look at the global numbers. Believe it or not, this disease was a leading cause of deaths globally in 2020, killing almost ten million people and accounting for almost one in every six deaths [52]!

Issues such as tobacco use, drinking alcohol, lack of physical activity, a high BMI, and low consumption of vegetables and fruit are attributed to around one third of cancer deaths, and in low and lower-middle-income countries, around thirty percent of cancer cases are attributed to cancer-causing infections [53].

Stress, or chronic stress specifically, has been linked to developing cancer due to anxiety, adversity, depression, and loneliness/social isolation, whereas acute stress, which is associated more with events happening in the short term, such as dealing with an emergency or a sudden attack, can often be beneficial to the body. Chronic stress is heavily connected to being a cause of ill health, potentially creating negative effects such as insomnia, gastro-intestinal disorders, depression, and anxiety, as well as an increased risk of cardiovascular disease, mental illness, and cancer [54].

As we know, a poor diet and a lack of exercise can lead to obesity. In 2021, a survey showed that an estimated 25.9% of adults in England were said to be obese, with 37.9% being overweight, and nearly 75% of 45-74-year-olds in England being in the category of being obese or overweight. In 2022, a survey was published showing that men were more likely to be in the category of being obese or overweight than women, with 45-74-year-olds most likely to be either obese or overweight [55];

45–54-year-olds - a combined percentage of 73%.
55–64-year-olds - a combined percentage of 72%.
65–74-year-olds - a combined percentage of 74%.
75+-year-olds   - a combined percentage of 69% [56].

The above percentages relate to obese and overweight people combined.

You can see a pattern emerging in relation to older people developing cancer with regards to weight and not being able to clear the body of damaged cells.

While I was having my pre-op in relation to my resection, a notice board caught my attention. It was referring to the maximum weight that the chairs in the waiting room could safely withstand! I pointed at the notice board and asked a passing nurse if they had ever had any chairs collapse. She sighed and said, 'We get some very big people in here.' I think the weight amounted to two of me – around 22 stone! You couldn't write it, could you? A weight warning for what looked like robust chairs! I was going to ask, 'Is that how bad it has gotten?' But it obviously had.

To make matters worse, let's look at the state of our children's health in relation to being overweight and obese. In England in 2024, it was reported that nearly a quarter of children aged ten and eleven were obese. It is said that around 60% to 85% of obese children will remain obese in adulthood. According to the most up-to-date information, when the obese and overweight figures were added together, 36.6% of children are an unhealthy weight [57]. What a start to life! Sadly, the problem starts even younger than that!

2014-2015 school year for 4-5-year-olds in England: 21.9% were overweight or living with obesity.
2022-2023 school year for 4-5-year-olds in England: 21.3% were overweight or living with obesity [58].

Ethnicity was shown to be a significant factor in relation to being overweight for both age groups in England (4-5-year-olds and 10-11-year-olds) [59].

In the UK, obesity and being overweight were the second-highest causes of cancer, and there are thirteen types of cancer linked to them: bowel, breast, thyroid, myeloma, meningioma, pancreatic, ovarian, kidney, oesophageal, womb, upper stomach, liver, and gallbladder [60].

So, how can these two conditions lead to cancer? It is down to the excess fat sending signals to other parts of our body, which can tell cells to divide more often, which, as we know, can lead to cancer developing. It is not a prerequisite that just because you are either obese or overweight that you will develop cancer; it is just more likely the more overweight you are and the longer you stay overweight for [61]. In other words, it is not helping your cause.

Visceral fat is found deep within the body, wrapped around our abdominal organs. Too much of this type of fat can increase the risk of developing aggressive prostate cancer, even in men with a low BMI. The risk increases the higher the BMI. It also raises the risk of developing breast cancer in women, along with other health issues, one of which is dementia! [62].

Earlier, I mentioned that substances and chemicals entering our bodies can trigger cancer. Here are some that have been listed by the NTP (National Toxicology Program) as known human carcinogens: arsenic, asbestos, benzene, benzidine, beryllium, cadmium, coal tar and coal-tar pitch, coke-oven emissions, ethylene oxide, formaldehyde, hexavalent chromium compounds, indoor emissions from the household combustion of coal, radon, soot, thorium, trichloroethylene, vinyl chloride, and wood dust [63].

A carcinogen is a substance that can cause cancer. However, it must be stated that just because a substance has been classified as a carcinogen, it does not necessarily mean that it will cause cancer. There are many factors that can have an influence on a person's development of cancer, such as duration of exposure, level of exposure, and the individual's genetic background [64]. There are a lot of variables involved, which is what makes it difficult to detect or gauge whether a person will develop it or not.

Let's face it, there are plenty of heavy smokers, heavy drinkers, and people who have a poor diet and exercise little who don't have cancer. Why don't they? They are prime candidates. Maybe it is related to age. Maybe when they get near the age of 65 or over, it will kick in? I don't know, but what I do know is that modern living is not helping us one bit. What I am going to talk about has nothing to do with food, drink, or exercise, but with the chemicals that we have surrounded ourselves with - chemicals that we have ended up breathing, eating, absorbing, and drinking every day of our lives.

It has been reported that there are over 350,000 synthetic chemicals, of which a very small amount has been evaluated for safety [65]. If only a very small number have been tested on an individual basis, one would assume that they haven't been tested in combinations. Many such chemicals are now hitting the headlines for the wrong reasons. In our rush to advance, we have failed to understand the consequences of unleashing all of these new chemicals and have created a toxic soup over which we have little understanding or control. The horse has well and truly bolted in this respect!

Some of these chemicals are called endocrine disruptors, which can disrupt the endocrine system. An endocrine disruptor can disrupt the functionality of a hormone, resulting in it over-responding, responding inappropriately, or blocking the effects of the hormone. It has been linked to problems such as increased cancer risk, developmental malformations, interference with reproduction, and disturbances in the nervous system and immune functions [66].

These chemicals are used in everyday products found at home and at work. They can be found in certain cosmetics, pesticides, herbicides, fragrances, the inner linings of canned food and drink, toys, food packaging, etc. [67]. I must stress that when I mention these products, I am not saying all of them, just that some products within those categories have been found to contain endocrine disruptors.

The problem for the consumer is understanding which products contain them, especially as products will be manufactured around the world, most likely to varying standards and formulations. I must admit to being baffled and astonished at the long list of ingredients listed on some food packaging, let alone trying to decipher what materials certain products are made from.

Let's have a look at a few of them:

PCBs (polychlorinated biphenyls) can be found in plastics, oil used in hydraulic systems, cable insulation, oil-based paints, tapes, adhesives, capacitors, transformers, and a variety of electrical equipment such as voltage regulators, switches, electromagnets, etc. PCBs are man-made organic chemicals that were manufactured between 1929 and 1979, when they were banned. They are not easily broken down in the environment, making them very long-lasting. PCBs were banned many years ago and, after being reassessed, were determined to be probable human carcinogens. Unfortunately, due to them being very long lasting, they can accumulate in the environment, in soil, and in food crops and can be ingested by small organisms and fish [68]. By eating things that have accumulated PCBs, we are more than likely contaminating ourselves.

You have to ask yourself: if something is classified as a probable human carcinogen, should it have even seen the light of day? What if probable human carcinogens turn out to be definite human carcinogens? It is a bit late by then, isn't it? Once they are out, they are out, and there is not much that can be done about it.

BPA (bisphenol A) has been found in items such as reusable water bottles, polycarbonate plastic, plastic and metal food packaging, and the internal linings of metal food containers. This chemical has been linked to cancer as well as mammary gland disease, lower sperm counts, behavioural changes, neurological toxicity, and immunotoxicity [69]. Worryingly, 95% of the adult population in the U.S. was found to have detectable levels of bisphenol A in their urine [70]! I must stress again that when I mention these products, I am not saying all of them, just that some products within those categories mentioned have been found to contain BPA.

We know that these harmful endocrine system disrupting chemicals can be found in plastics, so let's review plastic as a separate entity. There are many thousands of formulations of plastic, each providing a specific benefit. They are found pretty much everywhere you look and have served us well by providing many advantages over the materials that they have replaced.

The problem, as I see it, is that we have never fully controlled its growth, use, expansion, and what happens to it once it has served its purpose and is disposed of. This is not plastic's problem per se; it is ours; it is of our making. Knowing this, we still carry on developing new formulations in an effort to increase market share and profit.

Plastic has been around for over a century and keeps on increasing in volume produced as well as types. The irony is that early on, it was advertised as being a great material to make disposable cutlery and plates out of, as they could be just thrown away; no washing up!

Unfortunately, mankind has run before it could walk ever since the industrial revolution. We never really stop to understand the ramifications of our actions until it is too late, and then we spend a great deal of time and money trying to put our wrongs right. Plastic is a prime example.

Plastic has now been hitting the headlines for the wrong reasons: pollution, recycling (lack of it or its ineffectiveness), the fact that it is derived from oil, and health issues. The mention of microplastics and nanoplastics in particular has been making the headlines.

Over time, plastic eventually breaks down into smaller and smaller pieces: microplastics, which are less than 5mm in size, and nanoplastics, which are so small they cannot be seen by the human eye. These particles have been found in the soil in which we grow our food, the oceans where we catch the food that we eat, and the air that we breathe.

Gradually, chemicals can leach out of plastic and enter our bodies, causing serious health issues such as endocrine disruption, insulin resistance, decreased reproductive health, weight gain, and cancer [71]. Microplastics have even been found in human blood, saliva, kidneys, liver, placenta, breast milk, and an infant's first stool [72].

It is interesting to note, having written the above paragraph, that obesity, being overweight, and endocrine disruption have all been attributed to the development of cancer. I have to ask myself, 'Is the increasing trend of obesity and being overweight just down to eating the wrong food and lack of exercise, or is it a combination of that and the ingestion of plastic particles?'

Nanoplastics have also been linked to Parkinson's disease and other related dementias in that they could contribute to the risk and progression of this disease [73]. How worrying is that? If that is the case and we see production of plastics increasing over the coming years, it is going to have a devastating effect on all our lives.

Having read numerous articles, it appears that we are still learning about microplastics true effects on human health from a long-term perspective. We seem to have been slow on the uptake of what could be a massive health problem. Despite growing concerns over this, the volume of plastic produced is set to increase dramatically over the coming years.

The problem is that plastic is now so entrenched in our everyday lives that it is going to be incredibly difficult not to use it. After all, it is being used for specific beneficial reasons.

PFAS (per and polyfluoroalkyl substances) consist of around twelve thousand man-made chemicals, which are also known as forever chemicals due to their ability to last for thousands of years in our environment. These chemicals can be found in numerous industrial processes and a wide range of consumer products, such as food packaging, cookware, electronics, waterproof clothing, and furniture.[74].

These chemicals have been present in the environment since the 1940s, when they were first used in industry and the production of consumer products [75]. These chemicals are also said to bioaccumulate and biomagnify; some are toxic, with one in particular having a "probable link" to six diseases, of which kidney cancer and testicular cancer are two of them. The worst effects of these chemicals are usually found when people have been exposed to them due to them working in or living near a chemical plant producing such chemicals where leakage has occurred into the air, land, or local water supply [76].

Bioaccumulation is when an organism accumulates chemicals or toxins (usually man-made) in its body faster than it can excrete them or break them down. Biomagnification occurs when bioaccumulation is passed on up the food chain, e.g., when molluscs ingest toxic chemicals from the silt as they filter it, small fish eat the molluscs accumulating their toxins, a larger fish eats many of the smaller fish taking in higher doses of toxins, and an even larger fish eats that one. Each link in the chain towards the apex predator magnifies the amount of toxins taken in. In my mind, worryingly, humans are the apex predators on Earth!

Just to put it into perspective, in 2016, one study estimated that up to 23 million tonnes of plastic waste entered the world's aquatic ecosystems. As plastic breaks down into small particles, they sink to the bottom of the ocean and are eaten by crustaceans and fish. The consumption of these particles has led to an impaired reproductive rate, a slower swimming speed, an increase in stress, reduced absorption of nutrients, and death in larger species [77].

So not only have we overfished our oceans, decimating fish populations globally, but by allowing our waste to find its way into the ocean, we are also reducing marine life's ability to reproduce! One of our answers to this? To produce vast fish farms on land and at sea!

It is not only marine life that we are ingesting plastic by; it is sea salt too. It has been found in sea salt in the U.S., the U.K., China, France, and Spain [78].

We thought that eating seafood was good for us; maybe we need to think again. Maybe the concept of growing meat in a lab does make sense, seeing as though we seem to have contaminated the environment in which we and the animals that we eat live.

If you have a look on the Internet, there are countless articles in newspapers and government websites discussing the effects of PFAS. It gives you an idea of how bad the problem is and how out of control it has become, and this is just one type of chemical.

My point with regards to the above chemicals, along with hundreds of thousands of others, is that they are already present in our environment without our fully understanding the ramifications of our actions.

You would have thought that in the design process, the fact that some are virtually indestructible just might have raised a question as to whether they should be developed or not, and if they were to be developed, then they must be free of any link relating to the development of cancer or any other illness that could be harmful to human health. Surely that is plain old common sense and a wish to do the right thing? Isn't it?

There are countless endocrine disruptors - too many to write about. There are also countless arguments in relation to their effect on us. What I do know is that we seem to have introduced hundreds of thousands of chemicals into our environment, which are now polluting it and causing health problems for humans and wildlife alike. We have no idea as to what we have done, as we are still in the early stages of learning, and while we are learning about what we have done, we are introducing more and more of them.

I do not see humans being any different from wildlife in respect to bioaccumulation and biomagnification in that we spray our crops with insecticides and weed killers, and we breathe in pollution from combustion engines on a daily basis. As we eat our food, it is likely that we will digest some toxins as we do so. Now, we are obviously not eating each other as in the previous scenario, but we are at the top of the food chain; therefore, might it be the case that these toxins and chemicals are accumulating in our bodies and changing our genes at a cellular level?

If they are, then isn't it likely that the genetic changes could be passed on up the line, with every generation seeing an increase in altered cells, along with their own increasing exposure to these chemicals, adding to the possible gene changes of future generations? Is this how the number of affected people is increasing? With this in mind, let us have a quick look at something that can affect us on a daily basis: fumes from petrol-powered and diesel-powered vehicles.

Benzene is an 'aromatic' hydrocarbon found in vehicle exhaust emissions, although catalytic converters and a reduction in benzene in fuels have greatly reduced much of that element in the UK. It is also widely used in industry and in the chemical process to produce end products such as plastics, solvents, insecticides, foams, dyes, and detergents. Benzene has been classified as carcinogenic to humans (group 1) by the IARC, the International Agency for Research on Cancer. Worryingly, before its toxicity was known, benzene was used in the process of decaffeinating coffee as well as in some consumer products such as domestic cleaning solvents and cosmetics [79].

I sincerely hope that it is no longer used to decaffeinate coffee, as that is what I drink to combat my irritable bladder!

Diesel exhaust emissions, which are made up of soot particles, vapours, gases, and liquid aerosols, contain many carcinogens, one group of which is known as PAHs (polycyclic aromatic hydrocarbons) [80]. PAHs can be found in motor vehicle exhaust emissions, jet aircraft exhaust emissions, smoke from wood-burning stoves, smoke from forest fires, cigarette smoke, residential heating, and numerous industrial applications polluting all aspects of our environment – air, soil, and water. Numerous PAHs have properties such as being powerful immune suppressants, being toxic, and/or being carcinogenic (possible, probable, and known), and mutagenic [81]. A mutagen is something (a physical agent or substance) that is capable of causing mutation – the alteration of a cell's DNA sequence. It is not a good picture, is it?

The irony is that we were pushed towards using diesel due to it being more fuel efficient as well as producing less carbon dioxide. We were also incentivised by a lower car tax rate - lower emissions = lower tax. It is a double-edged sword, isn't it? Burning petrol produces more carbon dioxide, which contributes to global warming, and you get fewer mpg, but catalytic converters take out most of the benzene. On the other hand, burning diesel produces fewer greenhouse gas emissions, produces more mpg, but produces health-damaging pollutants.

So, is it going to be global warming or people's health? It kind of tells you the answer, doesn't it? We should be using neither! What we should have done was develop the electric car back in the 1800s. We had our chance, and we blew it!

Believe it or not, barbequing food on an open flame can be harmful because PAHs are created as well as HCAs (heterocyclic amines), which can end up coating the food. Using gas as a fuel is a better alternative than using either wood chips or charcoal. HCAs can also be mutagenic [82].

Later on, I look at processed meats and what is being said

about them. When you read about them, think about the type of food that you put on a barbecue. It is a double whammy, isn't it?

Not only do we breathe, drink, and eat from our environment, so do the animals and crops that we eat! I could write a book just about the chemicals that we have produced that are now roaming free in our environment and that are now having an adverse effect on human health. This is where I think both bioaccumulation and biomagnification come into play in relation to the increase in cancer. We have surrounded ourselves with chemicals that we eat, breathe, absorb, and drink that can be harmful to us - chemicals that we do not necessarily see, touch, or taste.

It is just another proving point in relation to running before we can walk in that we have introduced things that are toxic to us - things that we release into the environment with little thought or control. I have driven over one million miles in my career, and although my cars have had pollen filters, I dread to think of the fumes that I have inhaled during that time from both petrol-powered and diesel-powered vehicles.

A lot of comments that I have read communicate the fact that chemicals mainly affect people when they are exposed to them over an extended period of time and at higher doses than usual, e.g., when pollution has leaked into groundwater supplies or people have been exposed to chemicals during their work.

Could it be the case that even though the amount of exposure is low, our bodies are being exposed to so many chemicals at the same time that the sheer number of them is replacing the higher exposure of just one chemical? Could the exposure of so many chemicals at the same time, even at low levels, create a toxic soup that can trigger genetic changes within our bodies?

Can you remember the phrase 'don't dump on your own doorstep?' Well, we seem to have completely ignored our own advice. We now live in a toxic soup of chemicals that we know can be harmful to our health. We do not seem to have learnt either, as we are still producing and releasing new chemicals into our environment.

I think one of the worst descriptions that I have read is that of a chemical being a 'probable' carcinogen. Probable! I do not understand how and why we have allowed this to get so out of hand, or is it just the fact that we put growth and advancement first, even though it is killing us? If there is any doubt in relation to a chemical being carcinogenic, then the answer as to whether it should be used or not should be a resounding 'no,' not until it has been properly tested.

If rates of cancer are increasing across the population, then surely the cause of it must point to something that we are all exposed to. If we look at endocrine disrupting chemicals and carcinogenic chemicals from whatever source they come from, along with an increase in people living longer and obesity, I think that we might have our answer.

So, the million-dollar question is: can we beat cancer? There are countless organisations doing a sterling job in relation to fighting cancer, and with new treatments coming into play all the time, we are seeing better life expectancies for certain cancers. But can we actually stop cancer from happening in the first place?

I genuinely don't think we can, and I put that down to our dependence on chemicals, the lifestyle that we choose to live, the economic model of growth that we live by, how we seemingly prefer to try to right our wrongs rather than getting it right the first time, our reliance on medicines to cure us, and, ironically, a great health service allowing us to live longer. I think that we are too far down the road to change!

I think back to the book that I wrote in relation to humanity and the climate crisis. Part of the book looks at what humans have done in such a short period of time and why and how we do things. Part of the problem is that humanity has developed in such a short period of time (and is still developing at an alarming rate) in relation to our existence that Earth and nature have not had time to recalibrate themselves to enable them to cope with the changes, and that includes us.

We have bombarded our senses and bodies with too much too quickly, so much so that they have not had time to build a defence against the new paradigm. Our bodies are assaulted by thousands of chemicals, some of which we can now find embedded in our organs and travelling around in our blood, and yet knowing this, we carry on regardless, presumably in the belief that we will come up with a cure for what is happening to us.

We are said to be the most intelligent species on the planet. I am struggling to find one word to describe how I feel about the human race as a species. Is it ignorant? Arrogant? Stupid? Selfish? Greedy? Or is it all of them and more? A later paragraph explains why we won't stop. You can then decide which words you would use to best describe our species.

A classic example of this is wildlife not adapting fast enough to the changes in our weather and seasons, which have been driven by climate change. If you look at this on a smaller scale, our bodies and minds have not had time to adjust to the speed of our development either. We would have been better off staying as indigenous people and living a simpler, healthier life while maintaining a healthier, more respectful relationship with our environment and the wildlife in it.

I genuinely think that a lot of the mental health issues of today are related to the speed at which things have happened, are still happening, and are expected to happen. What this continual speed of advancement causes, in my mind, is stress.

We are all stressed at some point in our lives, but if you are constantly stressed (chronic stress) to the point of being depressed, lonely, or anxious, you could be increasing your risk of developing cancer. The reason why I have said this is that globally, almost one million new cancer cases in 2012 were partly attributed to stress in twenty- to thirty-nine-year-olds. This form of stress can encourage the transformation of healthy cells into cancer cells through the production of stress hormones, which can lead to the development of cancer. Changes to the body's immune function and inflammatory response caused by chronic stress, should they be long-term, are implicated in the development of cancer cells [83].

When you look at the state of affairs in 2023 and the three years prior to that, there has been an incredible amount of stress put on people around the world. Between the years of 2019 and 2023, the COVID-19 pandemic caused isolation, loneliness, fear, and stress as people feared for their and their loved ones' lives. The fact that rules had been imposed on us and that, within a week or so, the world had changed and we had no say in the matter was a cause of considerable stress for everyone.

On top of that, we have had to deal with the war between Ukraine and Russia, the cost-of-living crisis, teachers, doctors, and nurses striking, immigration, and the ongoing discussions relating to the climate crisis. The world is a mess! As the most intelligent creatures on the planet, how could we have gotten it so very wrong?

If you are young, I would say that there is an awful lot bearing down on your shoulders and little that you can do about it. I think even I, if I were young, would struggle to cope when you see the world burning; floods and droughts displacing millions of people; war and atrocities taking place along with their senselessness; increasing poverty; your parents maybe having to go to a food bank due to inflation; the increased cost of heating; and pandemics past and pending. It kind of makes you think, 'What is the point? What kind of future lies ahead of us?'

Thanks to the ever-increasing numbers and forms of digital communication, I don't think there has ever been so much pressure on people to 'keep up' with their 'friends' and to meet the supposed expectations of their peers. I find it a sad reflection in relation to what and how we think. I am not a fan of social media for many reasons, and I really couldn't give a rat's ass what people think of me.

Perhaps young people should stop trying to aspire to what they see on social media and concentrate on just being themselves and enjoying their lives. I have no doubt that it will help their mental health and, in doing so, their physical health in the long run.

To help counter stress, you need to maintain a positive attitude, have a healthy eating and drinking regime, exercise regularly, and find a way to combat your stress levels. It is easier said than done, isn't it, especially if you are on your own? Social interaction has always been an important part of human life. In my mind, social media should never be seen as a replacement for direct social interaction, because I don't think it is.

I underwent the most stress that I have ever felt at the end of my career and when I started my retirement. I had been working twelve- to sixteen-hour days for longer than I can remember, even taking and making calls when I was on holiday. I remember one time when we were on holiday in particular. We went on a boat trip around a lake, and I was on the phone to work for the duration of the forty-five-minute tour. When the tour finished, my partner said, 'You didn't see any of that, did you?' She went and bought two more tickets, banished me from using my phone, and we went on the tour again!

My stress levels were sky high during the last few months of work as I was desperately trying to put a large contract to bed. Having succeeded in what I wanted to achieve, I left satisfied that I had done everything that was needed.

Not long after starting retirement, my mother went into the early stages of dementia, which entailed me driving to see her due to her phoning me to tell me that she had a water leak, that there was something moving around in the roof, and that her fridge was leaking. There turned out to be no water leak; the 'thing' in her roof was in fact the smoke alarm beeping to indicate that its battery was getting low, and the fridge was not leaking; it was just a little condensation. When I opened it, I found it stuffed full of towels! These phone calls went on for months.

One of my worst visits was when I walked into her living room to find it full of flies. I asked mum what was going on, and she turned around and said, 'Look at all of these flies; they're just walking about.' To my horror, I saw what she had been doing – she had been squashing them with her fingers.

It is difficult to not get angry at the sight of your mum with squashed flies all over her fingers. It is at times like these that you realise how the tables have turned, in that I was looking after her as she did me when I was a child. It was her turn to get her own back for having to scrub the tar off my wiener, along with countless other misdemeanours.

Mum's dementia caused huge arguments within the family, and I can honestly say that I have never been so angry or stressed in my life. I just wanted to be left alone to recover from burnout, being both mentally and physically exhausted, and all I got when I was meant to be resting was a barrage of calls and hassle.

When things calmed down a bit, I started to help sort her out by taking her to the hospital, to an optician, to a foot specialist, to a hearing specialist, and helping to sort out and understand her finances. Around this time, my partner's father became ill with cancer, and I became very involved in that too. To add to my already mounting level of stress, my aunt also needed help with her dementia, and to top it all off, someone wrote off my beloved car. Welcome to retirement!

Unfortunately, due to the number of head traumas (besides going through a car windscreen) that I have experienced, I think that I am a prime candidate for this disease (dementia) because there have been numerous reports linking head trauma to both dementia and Alzheimer's.

I have quite a catalogue of head traumas, including being knocked off a motorcycle and being hurled over the roof of the car to land on my head. The worst part of this was that my motorcycle's petrol tank ruptured, leaving me lying in a pool of petrol. Thankfully, someone who lived close to me saw what had happened and pulled me out of it, although he did get a rollicking from the ambulance crew for moving me and taking my helmet off.

If it couldn't get any worse, it turned out that my mum was stuck in traffic just a few cars away! The irony was that a friend who I was going to meet also got knocked off his motorcycle, and so the injured and their parents all met in the hospital together.

The funniest head trauma that I experienced (if there is such a thing) was when I was in my teens. I climbed ten steps up the stairs at home to perform my impression of the Incredible Hulk. I psyched myself up and struck the pose, arms to the side and fists clenched. I let out a roar and jumped. What I did not account for was the overhang of the landing above.

I was concentrating so hard on landing safely, not breaking a leg or ankle, and not going through the glass door at the bottom of the stairs, that my forehead smashed into the rock-solid overhang, and I was knocked unconscious mid-jump. I woke up at the bottom of the stairs in a similar stance to a corpse with a chalk mark around it. I looked around to make sure that no one had seen me and struggled to my feet, holding my very sore head! We live and learn!

So, how long does cancer take to develop and show its ugly face? Well, there is no exact timeline, but it can happen over an extended timeframe. It can take as long as ten to fifteen years for a polyp to turn into cancer [84]

There is no answer as to when mine started, as it could have happened at any time, most likely while I was at work. What could have happened is that the levels of stress that I incurred after I retired could have exacerbated it, maybe accelerated it, or triggered it.

I will never know for sure, but the more that I read about it, the more I think that the way of life that we now live, which includes stress and many chemicals that we now find in our food, air, and water, has to be a large factor in cancer's progress.

Of course, there will always be an element of luck in relation to a person's genetic makeup as to whether it will or it won't lead to cells mutating. In that respect, there will always be an element of pot luck as to who will get it and who won't. All you can do is do your best by looking after your mental and physical health - do the right things for your body and mind.

12

Colon cancer and what causes it

So, are there different types of bowel cancer? There most certainly are:

Adenocarcinomas: this is the most common type of cancer, which starts in the bowel wall lining, which is what I had. The others listed below are rare compared to this one.

Squamous cell tumours: like the adenocarcinoma, the cancer starts in the bowel wall lining but affects the skin cells rather than the gland cells, as with the adenocarcinoma.

Carcinoid tumours: these are slow-growing and are found in hormone-producing tissue, normally in the digestive system.

Sarcomas: they are usually found in smooth muscle in the bowel and are called leiomyosarcomas.

Lymphomas: these are lymphatic system cancers.

Melanomas: these are types of skin cancer that can start in the rectum [85].

These are in addition to the many other disorders, irritations, and infections that can affect the digestive tract. There is a saying that a healthy gut means a healthy body and a healthy mind. I think, having read about the gut and cancer, that a healthy gut comes from a healthy body via a balanced diet, exercise, and sensible food intake, whereas a healthy mind comes from low stress, relaxation, fresh air, and a sensible work/life balance.

To keep the bowel healthy, we need to drink plenty of water, eat less saturated fat, and eat more fibre. Fibre activates the colon to move food through it by muscle contraction, which helps clear any leftovers that may slow things down. Saturated fats are associated with increased rates of colon diseases, so it is worth staying away from them and going for more healthy fats, such as Omega-3s found in oily fish. The colon needs water, as it helps lubricate and clean it as well as absorb left-over nutrients [86].

A very poignant piece of information is that nearly 30% of bowel cancer cases in the UK are caused by insufficient fibre [87]. It is a crying shame that we have all of this information and yet don't shout it out loud. Instead, we are told that eating too little fibre isn't good for us. It is not good enough; it is not a strong enough message. If I heard the above statistic, it would make me think again, especially when linked to colon cancer.

My partner now makes me a 'breakfast' every morning consisting of a bowl of sliced banana, blueberries, and fat free vanilla yogurt. It actually tastes very nice and contains fibre, delivers energy, and provides antioxidants, which help protect our cells and DNA from damage.

Out of 10 (10 being excellent and 1 being poor), how do you

score? I would say that before I had cancer, I scored one for fibre, one for saturated fats, and one for the amount of water that I drank. All in all, extremely poor! As you will read, I have altered my eating and drinking habits considerably since my first operation.

I think that we probably take our bowels too much for granted. It is an exceptionally complex organ that needs to be looked after. I suppose because it carries our waste, it is thought of as a garbage chute. Well, that garbage chute needs looking after by eating and drinking things that can maintain it. It is no different from making sure that your car is topped up with good-quality oil and is regularly serviced. Do not give your bowel a hard time because it may end up giving you one! It is a warning for us all.

One thing that I did after everything had settled down was to alter my diet and look at what was in our cupboards, fridge, and freezer. I started to throw away any processed or ultra-processed food that I found with nitrates or nitrites in it; these included packs of bacon, a tin of corned beef, a salami and pepperoni pizza, a tin of hot dogs, and some pate.

Nitrates and nitrites that have either been added to meat or produced whilst cooking meat can increase the risk of cancer. These chemicals can damage the cells that line the bowel, which can lead to bowel cancer [88].

I bought a water filter jug and started to drink plain water (nice and cold out of the fridge) instead of carbonated water

I drank good-quality fruit cordials rather than fizzy, sugary drinks; I reduced my chocolate and biscuit intake by around 75%; I stopped eating processed meat with nitrites or nitrates in it; and I ate more vegetables, fruit, and fibrous food (oat and honey cereal bars). I tried to create a more balanced diet, which would be good for my gut, as well as taking vitamin tablets (D3 and C), a cultured yoghurt drink containing vitamins D and B6, and turmeric tablets. Hopefully, some of these will bolster my immune system, and it is not too late to make a difference.

I was taken aback when I realised that some of the 'healthy' products that I was looking to buy to improve my diet actually contained as much salt as a bag of ready salted crisps and as much sugar as a chocolate biscuit. To make matters worse, some items had such a long list of ingredients that I had no idea what they were or what they did. It is worth a look to see what ingredients are listed and how much fat (especially saturated fat) and salt they have in them.

It is said that eating a Western diet, such as lots of sugary desserts, red meat, and processed foods, can increase the risk of developing colorectal cancer, whereas a diet that is concentrated on fruit, whole grains, nuts, beans, and vegetables is linked to a lower risk of colorectal cancer [89]. Knowing this, it is no surprise that obesity and being overweight can increase the risk of developing cancer. In the UK, more than one in twenty cases is due to these two factors, with thirteen cancers being caused by them [90].

Around 13% of all bowel cancer cases in the UK have been attributed to consuming lots of processed meat and red meat [91]. Processed meats are meats that have been preserved by curing, salting, smoking, or having preservatives added to them. A processed meat, for example, can be deli meats (salami, etc.), sausage, pate, corned beef, other canned meats, bacon, sliced luncheon meats, which include those with turkey and chicken in them, and ham [92].

As France is a large producer of such meats (charcuterie), they are taking this link to colon cancer very seriously, so much so that they were looking to put together an action plan to restrict the use of additives to only when strictly necessary [93]. In 2015, the WHO (World Health Organisation) showed the classification of red meat as Group 2a, meaning that it is probably carcinogenic to humans, whereas processed meat has the classification of Group 1, meaning that it is carcinogenic to humans [94].

The funny thing is, now that I think about it, when I was young, I remember people saying that they would not eat anything with preservatives or additives in it. It wasn't put as succinctly as that, but you get my drift. Now it has become the norm, and we seem to be paying the ultimate price for more choice, lower cost, and a longer shelf life - things that make our lives easier. Perhaps this is where the phrase 'convenience food' came to light?

Processed foods and ultra-processed foods are also in the headlines relating to whether they contribute to or cause cancer. One thing that is for sure is that if you are eating food that has a high fat content, specifically saturated fat, then there is a high risk of weight gain, and we know that being overweight or obese can be contributing factors to an increased risk of developing cancer.

I think a couple of key words in relation to the above paragraph and processed meats are 'lots of' and 'balance.' In most walks of life, you need to determine a balance - not too much and not too little. The same goes with your diet; be sensible about what you eat. If you want to learn more, visit the NHS website titled 'Red meat and the risk of bowel cancer.'

Globally, in 2020, it was reported that there had been a tripling of obesity since 1975. Believe it or not, over 70% of Qatar's population is classified as obese or overweight. In China, in 2002, 29% of adults were said to be overweight, and in 2020, it was reported that over 50% of adults were overweight (more than half a billion people), with 16.4% of these being obese! A changing diet (an increase in meat consumption and a low consumption of fruit), coupled with less exercise, were highlighted as causes [95].

It is a shame that we have so much information but do not seem to send the message home. I think it needs to be spelled out to young people so that they are fully aware of the ramifications of a poor diet, smoking, and little exercise. By spelled out, I mean discussions about cancer, chemotherapy, and how it affects not just you but your family and friends as well.

It should be hard-hitting; it should make them think and, more than think, act, so that they are doing the right thing. This could be a part of the curriculum - a topic within biology; it should be a part of the curriculum. If they do not know the whole picture, how can they understand it and act accordingly?

If we did this, would it make a difference? Are we strong enough to do something about it? I think, as a species, we seem to have lost the plot. We seem to have lost our discipline and self-control along with our ability to say no, whether it be in relation to food and drink consumption, gambling, gaming, vaping, or recreational drugs, which have all become addictions and need treatment.

Unfortunately, in my mind, we seem to be saying that being overweight is okay. The message that is being sent, as far as I understand it, is that we should embrace our bodies, be proud of them and who we are, and to not hide it, no matter how heavy you are. Is this really the message that we should be promoting on TV, which children also watch and learn from? I am not saying these people in these categories should be hidden or disgraced; what I am questioning is the celebrating, accepting, and embracing of it. It is not really the right message to be sending, is it?

To make matters worse, an element of political correctness has crept in, in that people are not calling people obese anymore; they are saying that they have obesity.

Obesity is costing the NHS a fortune (around £6.5 billion a year [96]), and it is only going to get worse the more we promote it as being normal and acceptable.

During my stays in the hospitals, I was surprised at the number of people who were either overweight or obese, but then should I have been, as they are both major contributors to illness. While I was having a coffee in a local supermarket, I looked around and realised that I, apart from the young cashier, was the only person who wasn't obese or overweight. It really does seem to have become the norm.

We should be tackling the root cause of it, not coming up with cures such as weight loss tablets, which people are now seemingly using as 'slimming' tablets! Prevention is better than cure. Isn't that right? The climate crisis is exactly the same; we are coming up with solutions but are not tackling the root cause, and that is why we will never beat it.

Obesity and being overweight are the same, in that they need to be tackled at root cause rather than after the event. We will need to carry on pumping billions into the NHS just to service these categories of people. As the money comes from taxes, we will either have to pay more taxes or see the waiting list keep on increasing, along with rates of cancer linked to these two categories.

I have said the same about climate change: young people

should be told about it, 'warts and all.' There is nothing worse than being told after the event. It is too late by then; the horse has already bolted, or in these instances, you have been diagnosed with cancer or your house has just been washed away due to flooding caused by climate change.

After I had written about climate change and humanity, I wanted to understand young people's perceptions relating to both topics. What did they think of them? Did they bother them? Did they know much about them? I contacted two schools and offered to conduct a Q&A session for sixteen- to eighteen-year-olds after school for those interested. Sadly, I didn't even receive a reply.

I understand that climate change is on the curriculum, but it is up to each individual school as to whether they include it or not. My main concern was the effect that it would have on the pupils. I did not want to cause them any more stress than they normally have, but these people are going to be the next politicians, police officers, industrialists, doctors, nurses, business managers, etc.

If we do not complete the picture for them, how can they act? It is a difficult one, isn't it? I think the same goes for cancer; they should know the complete picture so they can act accordingly, especially as it can take ten to fifteen years to come to light! Perhaps we should start screening much earlier too, as prevention is quicker and cheaper than cure. There is a definite story to be told here, and not one that just says that eating vegetables is good for you.

With increasing workloads and an imbalance between work and social time, the need for fast food increases, and this 'way of life' is already spreading to developing countries. As the population of these countries becomes wealthier, their diet will also change to foods that depict wealth and standing, along with increased consumption. Usually, this means an uptick in meat consumption.

An easy way to reduce food intake is to simply eat less, and to help you do this, you can make your portions smaller. It is easy to do at home, but not so easy when dining out. I have discussed portion sizes many times, even with restaurant owners and fish and chip shops.

Why have portion sizes increased so much? When I asked a restaurant owner why they didn't decrease the size of the main meal so that I could have a pudding or a starter and make themselves more money, I was told that it was what people expected now, and they would still have a three-course meal!

We have downsized as much as we can when ordering fish and chips. We started ordering a 'small' portion, and over time it grew to what was a normal portion - the same with the chips. We now share a small fish and chips between us and still end up throwing some in the bin! It is crazy. No wonder obesity is on the rise. People just do not seem to be able to say no or leave food on their plates.

When I was out driving, I found motorway service stations

no better. I used to go in and buy a couple of chocolate bars and a fizzy drink, only to be accosted by the cashier, who was trying to sell me a chocolate bar that was three times the size of what I had chosen for just £1. Promoting two chocolate bars for £1 was also a favourite. I am afraid that this is the price that we pay for economies of scale in manufacturing and global competition. It doesn't help our situation, does it? It just inflames it.

I am afraid that the way manufacturing businesses are run nowadays is orientated around efficiency, economies of scale (the more you produce, the cheaper it is), and competition. This means that competition drives the price down between manufacturers and retailers, and efficiency and economies of scale mean a cheaper production cost; therefore, lots of cheap products are manufactured and need to be sold, hence the deals that can be offered (two for one, etc.).

As I said in my first book, 'You don't get something for nothing; there is always a trade-off.' In this instance, we appear to have traded more choice, a longer shelf life, and cheaper products for an increase in illnesses and cancer. However, it has been our choice; we have the option of avoiding inflammatory diets and eating too much, but we appear to ignore it.

Maybe the sheer number of TV programs and advertisements relating to food and cooking doesn't help, nor do the videos of people eating as much food as they can in as short a time as possible. Call me old-fashioned, but for the life of me, I cannot understand the pleasure or interest in watching someone cram food into their mouth as fast as they can.

This is how it is in pretty much every walk of life, so how do we stop it? How do we stop being offered cheaper products and more choice? We cannot, because we are driven by growth; we know nothing else. One of the reasons I have alluded to this is that the more products we make, the more pollution we produce, and the more chemicals we will come into contact with. We are on a giant hamster wheel with no visible exit.

Just to prove a point. I went onto a large retailer's website to find 106 choices of toothpaste. 106! When I was in DIY retail in the 80s, we gave a choice of three per item. We offered a cheap one, an expensive one, and a middle-of-the-road one. Do we really need so much choice?

When you look at our diet and the extra ingredients that we are putting in our food for flavour and to increase shelf life, coupled with the toxic mix of chemicals that we have introduced that we come into contact with every day and the stressful lives that we lead, it is no wonder that we are suffering with such high rates of cancer and illness.

As we know no better than growth and the 'advancement' of our species, we will not stop doing what we are doing. The sad thing is that this is the scenario that developing countries are heading into - some are already there, and in such a short time! Growth is literally killing us.

13

What is the future of colon cancer treatment?

Let us look at what is happening to try and tackle colon cancer and other cancers; hopefully, it will spread a ray of sunshine over what is a gloomy topic. Cancer treatments are advancing all the time, but one of the key weapons in tackling it is testing; finding the cancer in its early stages can mean a better prognosis. It can mean a better prognosis and can also save the NHS valuable time and money with regard to costly treatment.

One thing that can be done is to have chemotherapy before the operation. The aim is to shrink the tumour, which should mean less surgery or make it easier to remove all of the cancer. This could also lead to a smaller area of your body receiving radiotherapy [97]. It has been found that there is a 28% reduction in the risk of colon cancer returning if this treatment is used in the early stages [98]. Very precise radiotherapy is also looking to be used before the operation takes place in relation to brain tumours to reduce the probability of them returning quickly [99].

A liquid biopsy is a way of discovering very small fragments of DNA in the blood that have been released from cancer cells. The idea behind this is to be able to detect cancers (ten of them) before people show symptoms [100]. The next step from this is to use a liquid biopsy to detect genetic faults in someone's cancer so that personalised medicines can be offered, as well as try to match patients who have exhausted all other means to clinical trials by understanding the genetic faults in their cancer. The hope is that this service will be offered as part of routine NHS care if large-scale trials prove successful [101]. I would have thought that the incorporation of AI (artificial intelligence) would be a very useful tool for this kind of application.

As cancer is a gene-based disease, it would seem logical to look at tackling it from a gene-based perspective. With this in mind, much work is being done, and as part of a gene therapy programme, viruses are being engineered to replicate within cancer cells and kill them [102]. To me, this sounds a little bit like what phage do: they replicate inside a bacterium cell and destroy the cell membrane, or they replicate their genes into the bacterium genome to then be transmitted to future generations [103].

Out of interest, I looked on the Internet, and lo and behold, there is a lot of research being conducted as to how phage can help fight cancer. Phage can be manipulated genetically to target very specific cells without damaging others. I would say the use of phage is much more targeted than chemotherapy. There are numerous links in the 'Useful links' section at the end of the book that relate to phage.

Our body is home to trillions of microorganisms, which include bacteria, fungi, and viruses; this is called our microbiome, with our gut holding a significant portion of it. Interestingly, a bacterium called Fusobacterium has been found in approximately one-third of bowel cancers. It is thought that this particular bacterium is most likely to be found in people who eat what is called an inflammatory diet and is more frequently found in cancers of the right side of the colon [104]. Mine was on the right-hand side.

You have guessed it: an inflammatory diet consists of all the things that are said to be bad for you: red and processed meat, ultra-processed food, added sugar, trans fats, omega-6 fatty acids, refined carbohydrates such as bread, crackers, chips, white rice, and sugary cereals [105].

Understanding the relationship between the microbiome and cancer is a huge task, as there are so many types of bacteria in the gut, and scientists need to understand what they all do and how they interact with other microbes, the immune system, or each other. To make matters even more complicated, the microbiome can vary from person to person and even between nations [106].

The gut's microbiome is in fact the biggest immune system organ in our body, containing up to 80% of the body's immune cells; it can train the immune system; byproducts of helpful gut bacteria have anti-inflammatory properties relevant to the gut; and it is the largest endocrine system organ in our body. Pollutants, alcohol, tobacco smoke, processed foods, foods with a high sugar level, and foods with a high level of saturated fat can all harm the microbiome [107].

Having written the above paragraph, it is obvious why it is so important to keep the gut microbiome healthy by eating a balanced diet containing fruit, nuts, and vegetables, as these help to protect it by promoting healthy microbes. It has to be a balance. We cannot sit back and rely on the advancement of medicine and treatments for cancer; we must do our bit. It is all there to read and understand.

Unfortunately, we are introducing things into our microbiome that it has never had to deal with before. Our gut needs time to evolve and be able to protect itself against all of the new chemicals and ingredients that it is now coming into contact with.

It isn't just the case that we are introducing new elements to our microbiome; it is also the fact that we are overloading it with them at the same time.

In my first book, I list important things that have happened in humanity's history, such as the development of the internal combustion engine, the telephone, the jet engine, space travel, landing on the moon, etc., and I ask the reader to keep this in the back of their minds whilst reading the book. The fact is, all of these life changing developments have happened in less than two hundred years! Our bodies and minds haven't changed in that time, have they? Yet we are meant to cope with all of this monumental change both physically and mentally in the way in which we live our lives.

Targeted and immunotherapy drugs are also being used in the

fight against advanced colon cancer (when it has spread from the colon or rectum to elsewhere in the body). Targeted drugs look for the difference between normal cells and cancer cells by way of how they survive and grow to enable them to target cancer cells, whereas immunotherapy drugs help attack cancer by helping the immune system. Both of these treatments are designed to manage the cancer (slowing the growth down or shrinking the tumour), but they cannot usually cure it [108].

If you wish to take part in a trial, there are many clinical trials taking place that you can apply to be a part of [109]. There are numerous trials just for colon cancer [110]. There are also numerous links in the 'Useful links' section at the back of the book that relate to trials.

There is a tremendous amount of work being carried out with regards to finding cancer at its very early stage, treating it once it has taken hold, and extending life should the disease become advanced. For me, the concept of using genetically modified phage is an idea that really excites me, as they are so bespoke in what they do and are so targeted. I think it is a shame that we (the West) didn't carry on developing bacteriophage at the same time that we discovered and developed antibiotics; that way, we would have an even more formidable arsenal to tackle infections and diseases with.

Unfortunately, I feel that the cancer crisis that we find ourselves in is man-made, just as the climate crisis that we now find ourselves in is. In fact, I feel the two are linked and have the same causes. Where our increasing consumption, due to competition driving increased and more efficient manufacturing, creates more and more emissions, it also generates more and more pollution and cheaper products.

As the world is geared for growth and as the global population carries on increasing, we find ourselves trapped in this giant hamster wheel of growth, which drives consumption (food included), pollution (endocrine disruptors, industrial discharges, vehicle pollution, etc.), stress, and, I think invariably, cancer.

Our biggest problem, and one that I do not see us addressing, is how do we stop growth or at least start to slow it down, as our society is founded on it, and how do we stop using all of the toxic chemicals that are now so embedded in everyday life to slow down the increase of the toxic soup of chemicals that we have created and in which we live? This has got to be the biggest and most important question to face mankind since it first evolved. The sad thing is that everything that I see and hear is still geared towards growth, despite us facing the biggest crises that we have ever faced. We are literally killing ourselves to live.

Having said all of that, I feel that the ball is still firmly in our court. We have the knowledge and the ability to help prevent developing this disease, as we know that eating certain foods is bad for us and that eating certain foods is good for us. We also know that obesity, being overweight, a lack of exercise, and chronic stress have a say in the matter. With regards to pollution and chemicals that are maybe, probably, definitely carcinogenic, there is not an awful lot that we can do on a personal level apart from try to be aware of them and to stay away from them.

What we cannot and must not do is leave it to our healthcare providers and scientists to come up with a magic cure. We have to do our bit. We must do our bit. After all, it is in everyone's interest to do so, especially with our health service and its employees under such stress. I suppose at the end of the day, the question has to be, 'How much do you value your life, and how bothered are you in relation to what happens to our health service and its employees?'

Useful links

Among the following links, numerous trials have been listed. I would suggest that it is up to each individual to liaise with their medical team first should they want to discuss the possibility of taking part in a trial should they think they need to. Some of the links are from countries outside the UK. The links are for information only.

Their inclusion does not mean that the author is endorsing any companies, organisations, or treatments mentioned. They have been included for information only.

Please note that all Internet links have been provided in good faith and have been visited using a computer with up-to-date antivirus software. They have been successfully visited by the author with no warning issued relating to any form of malware or virus being present at the time of visiting; therefore, the publisher accepts no responsibility, liability, or indemnity against loss of any kind, as it is the individual's decision to take the risk as to whether they visit the site or not.

Due to websites being updated, you may find some of the links are no longer accessible. If this is the case, one can search the Internet using some of the information contained within the link, such as the organisation's name and the topic. You might find more up-to-date information available.

https://leicesterbrc.nihr.ac.uk/centre-for-phage-research/

https://nexabiome.com/blog/bacteriophages-in-cancer-therapy-current-research-and-future-perspectives/

https://www.thecancerscreeningtrust.co.uk/

https://www.macmillan.org.uk/cancer-information-and-support/bowel-cancer/colon-cancer

https://www.bowelresearchuk.org

https://www.bowelcanceruk.org.uk/

https://www.cancerresearchuk.org/our-research-by-cancer-type/our-research-into-bowel-cancer

https://www.nhs.uk/conditions/bowel-cancer/

https://www.royalmarsden.nhs.uk/your-care/cancer-types/gastrointestinal/lower-gastrointestinal/colorectal-cancer

https://www.who.int/news-room/fact-sheets/detail/colorectal-cancer

https://www.cancerresearchuk.org/about-cancer/bowel-cancer/treatment/research-clinical-trials

https://www.royalmarsden.nhs.uk/about-royal-marsden/our-research/clinical-trials

https://www.ucl.ac.uk/news/2021/may/clinical-trial-co-led-ucl-leads-new-bowel-cancer-drug-approval

https://www.mcrc.manchester.ac.uk/trial-drug-helps-rectal-cancer-patients-avoid-surgery/

https://crukcambridgecentre.org.uk/patient-care/clinical-research/colorectal

https://www.royalsurrey.nhs.uk/news/launch-of-groundbreaking-international-cancer-vaccine-trial-10320/

https://www.leeds.ac.uk/news-health/news/article/5231/remarkable-results-in-colon-cancer-trial

https://www.uclh.nhs.uk/our-services/find-service/cancer-services/cancer-clinical-trials

https://cmcanceralliance.nhs.uk/news/new-clinical-trial-giving-hope-people-bowel-cancer-merseyside

https://www.qub.ac.uk/research-centres/cancer-research/News/Groundbreakingresearchcouldrevolutionisehowbowelcanceristreated-1.html

https://flipbooks.leedsth.nhs.uk/LN003907.pdf

https://bepartofresearch.nihr.ac.uk/

https://www.christie.nhs.uk/about-us/news-at-the-christie/latest-news-stories/sheffield-woman-celebrates-6-years-of-successful-experimental-bowel-cancer-treatment

https://www.england.nhs.uk/2024/05/thousands-of-nhs-patients-to-access-trials-of-personalised-cancer-vaccines/

https://www.acpgbi.org.uk/professionals/research_audit/trials/uk_colorectal_trials.aspx

https://www.mskcc.org/news/rectal-cancer-disappears-after-experimental-use-immunotherapy

https://www.ucl.ac.uk/news/2024/jun/immunotherapy-significantly-increases-number-patients-free-bowel-cancer

https://www.bowelcanceruk.org.uk/news-and-blogs/news/clinical-trials-recruiting-bowel-cancer-patients-across-the-uk/

https://sbuhb.nhs.wales/news/swansea-bay-health-news/first-person-in-wales-to-get-cancer-wonder-drug-is-given-the-all-clear/

https://www.clinicaltrialsregister.eu/ctr-search/search?query=Colon%2FRectal+Cancer+Colon+Cancer

https://www.cancerresearch.org/cancer-types/colorectal-cancer

https://www.aru.ac.uk/news/successful-trial-for-new-colorectal-cancer-treatment

https://www.sciencedaily.com/releases/2024/06/240614141852.htm

https://www.hcahealthcare.co.uk/Blog/A-new-era-in-bowel-cancer-treatment

https://link.springer.com/article/10.1007/s00018-024-05174-7#:~:text=Photodynamic%20therapy%20(PDT)%20represents%20an,a%20disulfide%2Dconstrained%20peptide%20nonamer.

https://www.ncbi.nlm.nih.gov/pmc/articles/PMC10684691/

https://www.frontiersin.org/journals/immunology/articles/10.3389/fimmu.2022.957233/full

https://www.ukphagetherapy.org/#:~:text=Patients%20in%20the%20UK%20must,phage%20therapy%20should%20be%20considered.

https://immucura.com/?gad_source=1&gclid=EAIaIQobChMIo4Tvr-iFiAMVHpVQBh2RhghEEAAYAiAAEgJ9svD_BwE

https://www.imperial.ac.uk/news/190727/tumour-targeting-viruses-hold-hope-incurable-brain/

https://www.gosh.nhs.uk/news/first-use-pioneering-phage-virus-therapy-treat-patient-cystic-fibrosis/

https://ukhsa.blog.gov.uk/2024/03/12/how-bacteria-munching-viruses-could-offer-an-alternative-to-antibiotics/

https://www.cancerresearchuk.org/about-cancer/bowel-cancer/survival

https://www.webmd.com/colorectal-cancer/news/20240314/new-blood-test-colon-cancer-highly-accurate-trial

https://www.webmd.com/colorectal-cancer/news/20230321/cm/this-common-infection-could-raise-your-risk-for-colon-cancer

https://www.cancercenter.com/cancer-types/colorectal-cancer/types/metastatic-colorectal-cancer

https://www.cancer.gov/types/colorectal/research#:~:text=In%20January%202023%2C%20the%20Food,of%20a%20protein%20called%20HER2.

https://www.bowelcanceruk.org.uk/news-and-blogs/research-blog/what-is-the-new-advanced-bowel-cancer-drug-that-has-been-approved-by-nice/

https://www.bowelcanceruk.org.uk/news-and-blogs/news/new-research-hailed-as-%E2%80%98promising%E2%80%99-for-thousands-with-advanced-bowel-cancer/

Reference section

This section provides reference points as to where certain information was found. There will be a small number next to the end of a sentence or paragraph. If you look for that number below, there is a link to the website where you can read more about the particular topic of interest. The date next to the link refers to the date shown on the particular page as to when it was last amended when read, or if that was not available, I have written the date when it was read by myself.

This reference section recognises and pays homage to the publications, organisations, and authors who have published such valuable information. A huge thank you to all those listed below. I hope that you find their articles as interesting and informative as I did.

---

[1] https://www.bowelcanceruk.org.uk/about-bowel-cancer/symptoms/ July 2022

[2] https://www.nhs.uk/conditions/bowel-cancer-screening/ 8th November 2021

[3] https://www.nhs.uk/conditions/blood-in-urine/ 24th June 2020

[4] https://www.esht.nhs.uk/service/cancer-services/urgent-suspected-cancer/ 27th February 2020

[5] https://www.nhs.uk/conditions/bladder-cancer/symptoms/ 1st July 2021

[6] https://www.ncbi.nlm.nih.gov/books/NBK507857/ 1st August 2022

[7] https://www.cancer.gov/publications/dictionaries/cancer-terms/def/small-intestine Read on 9th February 2023

[8] https://www.healthdirect.gov.au/polyps July 2022

[9] https://www.ncbi.nlm.nih.gov/pmc/articles/PMC3981256/ 30th May 2011

[10] https://www.bowelcanceruk.org.uk/about-bowel-cancer/diagnosis/staging-and-grading/ June 2019

[11] https://www.cancer.org/treatment/understanding-your-diagnosis/lymph-nodes-and-cancer.html 2nd March 2021

[12] https://www.cancer.org/treatment/understanding-your-diagnosis/lymph-nodes-and-cancer.html 2nd March 2021

[13] https://www.cancer.gov/types/metastatic-cancer#:~:text=Cancer%20that%20spreads%20from%20where,stage%20IV%20(4)%20cancer. 10th November 2020

[14] https://www.cdc.gov/sepsis/about/?CDC_AAref_Val=https://www.cdc.gov/sepsis/what-is-sepsis.html 8th March 2024

[15] https://www.macmillan.org.uk/cancer-information-and-support/bowel-cancer/what-is-a-stoma 30th April 2020

[16] https://sthk.merseywestlancs.nhs.uk/media/.leaflets/614b14b7e1a f23.65792202.pdf Read on 22nd August 2023

[17] https://www.esneft.nhs.uk/leaflet/bowel-surgery-right-hemicolectomy/ 1st April 2022

[18] https://www.mayoclinic.org/diseases-conditions/cancer/in-depth/cancer-diagnosis/art-20046459 10th March 2022

[19] https://www.exeterlaboratory.com/test/carcinoembryonic-antigen-cea/ 12th March 2019

[20] https://www.mayoclinic.org/diseases-conditions/cancer/in-depth/cancer-diagnosis/art-20046459 10th March 2022

[21] https://www.mayoclinic.org/diseases-conditions/cancer/in-depth/cancer-diagnosis/art-20046459 10th March 2022

[22] https://www.newcastle-hospitals.nhs.uk/services/radiology/ct-scans/ 18th February 2021

[23] https://www.nhs.uk/conditions/ct-scan/ 8th November 2023

[24] https://my.clevelandclinic.org/health/diseases/22324-anastomotic-leak.02/03/22. Read on 2nd June 2023

[25] https://my.clevelandclinic.org/health/treatments/14791-intermittent-pneumatic-compression-ipc-device 18th April 2023

[26] https://www.heartspecialistsgroup.com/the-circulatory-system-and-the-second-heart/ Read on 2nd June 2023

[27] https://www.hollandandbarrett.com/the-health-hub/conditions/heart-health/circulation/what-is-a-normal-body-temperature/ Read on 2nd June 2023

[28] https://www.sepsis.org/sepsis-basics/symptoms/ Read on 2nd June 2023

[29] https://www.cancerresearchuk.org/about-cancer/treatment/chemotherapy/planning/your-chemotherapy-plan 2nd July 2020

[30] https://www.cancerresearchuk.org/about-cancer/treatment/chemotherapy/side-effects/dpd-deficiency 26th October 2020

[31] https://www.macmillan.org.uk/cancer-information-and-support/treatments-and-drugs/steroids 1st February 2022

[32] https://www.cancerresearchuk.org/about-cancer/treatment/drugs/oxaliplatin-eloxatin 13th January 2023

[33] https://www.cancerresearchuk.org/about-cancer/bowel-cancer/risks-causes 3rd December 2021

[34] https://www.nhs.uk/conditions/cancer/ 13th October 2022

[35] https://www.macmillan.org.uk/cancer-information-and-support/secondary-liver-cancer/treatment-for-secondary-cancer-in-the-liver 30th June 2020

[36] https://www.macmillan.org.uk/cancer-information-and-support/treatments-and-drugs/immunotherapy 1st August 2022

[37] https://britishlivertrust.org.uk/information-and-support/liver-health-2/abouttheliver/ Read on 10th July 2024

[38] https://www.cancer.gov/about-cancer/diagnosis-staging/diagnosis/tumor-grade 1st August 2022

[39] https://www.cancer.gov/about-cancer/diagnosis-staging/diagnosis/tumor-grade 1st August 2022

[40] https://acsjournals.onlinelibrary.wiley.com/doi/10.3322/canjclin.54.6.295 Read on 16th August 2024.

[41] https://www.cancerresearchuk.org/sites/default/files/cancer_in_the_uk_report-overview-03.pdf Read on 8th August 2024

[42] https://www.independent.co.uk/news/uk/cancer-cases-rise-uk-nhs-b2274977.html 3rd February 2023

[43] https://www.cancerresearchuk.org/health-professional/cancer-statistics/worldwide-cancer#heading-Zero Read on 8th August 2024

[44] https://www.nhs.uk/conditions/cancer/ 13th October 2022

[45] https://www.nhs.uk/conditions/cancer/ 13th October 2022

[46] https://www.nhs.uk/conditions/cancer/ 13th October 2022

[47] https://www.cancer.gov/about-cancer/understanding/what-is-cancer 11th October 2021

[48] https://www.cancer.org/healthy/cancer-causes/infectious-agents/infections-that-can-lead-to-cancer/viruses.html 21st March 2023

[49] https://www.bma.org.uk/advice-and-support/nhs-delivery-and-workforce/pressures/nhs-backlog-data-analysis 8th August 2024

[50] https://blog.ons.gov.uk/2019/04/26/are-there-more-people-diagnosed-with-cancer/ 26th April 2019

[51] https://www.cancer.gov/about-cancer/understanding/what-is-cancer 11th October 2021

[52] https://www.who.int/news-room/fact-sheets/detail/cancer 3rd February 2022

[53] https://www.who.int/news-room/fact-sheets/detail/cancer 3rd February 2022

[54] https://www.ncbi.nlm.nih.gov/pmc/articles/PMC7466429/ 19th August 2020

[55] https://commonslibrary.parliament.uk/research-briefings/sn03336/ 12th January 2023

56 https://commonslibrary.parliament.uk/research-briefings/sn03336/ 12th January 2023

57 https://www.theguardian.com/society/2024/jan/24/child-obesity-in-england-still-above-pre-pandemic-levels-study-finds 24th January 2024

58 https://www.ethnicity-facts-figures.service.gov.uk/health/diet-and-exercise/overweight-children/latest/ 11th July 2024

59 https://www.ethnicity-facts-figures.service.gov.uk/health/diet-and-exercise/overweight-children/latest/ 11th July 2024

60 https://www.cancerresearchuk.org/about-cancer/causes-of-cancer/bodyweight-and-cancer/how-does-obesity-cause-cancer 14th February 2023

61 https://www.cancerresearchuk.org/about-cancer/causes-of-cancer/bodyweight-and-cancer/how-does-obesity-cause-cancer 14th February 2023

62 https://www.pcf.org/c/body-fat-and-your-risk-of-dying-of-prostate-cancer/ Read on 12th July 2024

63 https://www.cancer.gov/about-cancer/causes-prevention/risk/substances 17th June 2022

64 https://www.cancer.gov/about-cancer/causes-prevention/risk/substances 17th June 2022

65
https://www.theguardian.com/environment/2022/jan/18/chemical-pollution-has-passed-safe-limit-for-humanity-say-scientists 18th January 2022

66 https://www.epa.gov/endocrine-disruption/overview-endocrine-disruption#chemicals 13th March 2023

67
https://www.niehs.nih.gov/health/topics/agents/endocrine/index.cfm 2nd June 2023

68 https://www.epa.gov/pcbs/learn-about-polychlorinated-biphenyls-pcbs 12th April 2023

69 https://www.theguardian.com/us-news/2022/feb/06/americans-exposed-toxic-bpa-fda-study 6th February 2022

[70] https://www.theguardian.com/environment/2017/sep/08/sea-salt-around-world-contaminated-by-plastic-studies 8th September 2017

[71] https://www.undp.org/kosovo/blog/microplastics-human-health-how-much-do-they-harm-us 5th June 2023

[72] https://magazine.hms.harvard.edu/articles/microplastics-everywhere Spring 2023. Read on 26th July 2024

[73] https://www.nih.gov/news-events/nih-research-matters/nanoplastics-may-help-set-stage-parkinson-s-risk 12th December 2023

[74] https://www.theguardian.com/environment/2023/feb/23/what-are-pfas-forever-chemicals-how-toxic-are-they-and-how-do-you-become-exposed 23rd February 2023

[75] https://www.atsdr.cdc.gov/pfas/health-effects/overview.html 18th January 2024

[76] https://www.theguardian.com/environment/2023/feb/23/what-are-pfas-forever-chemicals-how-toxic-are-they-and-how-do-you-become-exposed 23rd February 2023

[77] https://restoreactscienceprogram.noaa.gov/miscellaneous/microplastics-in-deep-sea-stomachs-study-finds-plastic-eaten-by-fish-and-crustaceans-increases-with-depth-in-the-gulf-of-mexico 24th July 2023

[78] https://www.theguardian.com/environment/2017/sep/08/sea-salt-around-world-contaminated-by-plastic-studies 8th September 2017

[79] https://www.gov.uk/government/publications/benzene-general-information-incident-management-and-toxicology/benzene-general-information 14th August 2019

[80] https://www.hse.gov.uk/construction/healthrisks/cancer-and-construction/diesel-engine-exhaust.htm Read on 15th June 2023

[81] https://www.sciencedirect.com/science/article/pii/S111006211420 0237 March 2016, read on 15th June 2023

[82] https://www.bbc.co.uk/food/articles/barbecue_cooking_risks Read on 15th June 2023

83 https://www.ncbi.nlm.nih.gov/pmc/articles/PMC7466429/ 19th August 2020

84 https://www.cancer.org/cancer/colon-rectal-cancer/detection-diagnosis-staging/detection.html 29th June 2020

85 https://www.cancerresearchuk.org/about-cancer/bowel-cancer/stages-types-and-grades/types 11th January 2022

86 https://my.clevelandclinic.org/health/body/22134-colon-large-intestine 12/08/2021. Read on 15th June 2023

87 https://www.cancerresearchuk.org/about-cancer/bowel-cancer/risks-causes 3rd December 2021

88 https://www.cancerresearchuk.org/about-cancer/causes-of-cancer/diet-and-cancer/does-eating-processed-and-red-meat-cause-cancer 26th July 2023

89 https://www.cancer.org/research/acs-research-highlights/nutrition-and-physical-activity-research-highlights/exploring-how-food-choices-influence-the-risk-for-colon-cancer.html Read on 15th June 2023

90 https://www.cancerresearchuk.org/about-cancer/causes-of-cancer/bodyweight-and-cancer/how-does-obesity-cause-cancer 14th February 2023

91 https://www.cancerresearchuk.org/about-cancer/bowel-cancer/risks-causes 3rd December 2021

92 https://www.nhs.uk/live-well/eat-well/food-guidelines-and-food-labels/red-meat-and-the-risk-of-bowel-cancer/ 15th March 2021

93 https://www.theguardian.com/world/2022/jul/12/charcuterie-link-colon-cancer-confirmed-french-authorities 12th July 2022

94 https://www.who.int/news-room/questions-and-answers/item/cancer-carcinogenicity-of-the-consumption-of-red-meat-and-processed-meat 26th October 2015

95 https://www.bbc.co.uk/news/world-asia-china-55428530 23rd December 2020

96 https://healthmedia.blog.gov.uk/category/public-health/obesity/ 2nd February 2024

97 https://www.cancerresearchuk.org/about-cancer/treatment/chemotherapy/when-you-might-have-chemotherapy 11th June 2020

98 https://www.theguardian.com/society/2023/jan/19/new-treatment-strategy-cuts-risk-of-bowel-cancer-returning-by-28 19th January 2023

99 https://www.theguardian.com/science/2023/feb/02/pioneering-nhs-trial-targets-brain-tumours-before-surgery-radiotherapy 2nd February 2023

100 https://www.theguardian.com/society/2018/jun/01/doctors-welcome-possible-holy-grail-of-cancer-research 1st June 2018

101 https://www.theguardian.com/society/2022/jan/31/nhs-cancer-patients-to-get-pioneering-genetic-test-to-find-best-treatments 31st January 2022

102 https://www.bartscancer.london/our-research/cancer-gene-therapy/ Read on 12th April 2023

103 https://www.ncbi.nlm.nih.gov/pmc/articles/PMC7923149/ 17th February 2021

104 https://news.cancerresearchuk.org/2019/03/21/could-the-bacteria-in-our-gut-help-treat-cancer/ 21st March 2019

105 https://health.clevelandclinic.org/5-foods-that-can-cause-inflammation/ 15th June 2020

106 https://news.cancerresearchuk.org/2019/03/21/could-the-bacteria-in-our-gut-help-treat-cancer/ 21st March 2019

107 https://my.clevelandclinic.org/health/body/25201-gut-microbiome 18th August 2023

108 https://www.cancerresearchuk.org/about-cancer/bowel-cancer/advanced/treatment/targeted-cancer-drugs-treatment 3rd February 2023

109 https://www.cancerresearchuk.org/about-cancer/find-a-clinical-trial/how-to-join-a-clinical-trial 1st February 2022

110 https://www.cancerresearchuk.org/about-cancer/bowel-cancer/treatment/research-clinical-trials/research-diagnosing-treating-bowel-cancer 6th February 2023